MW00952620

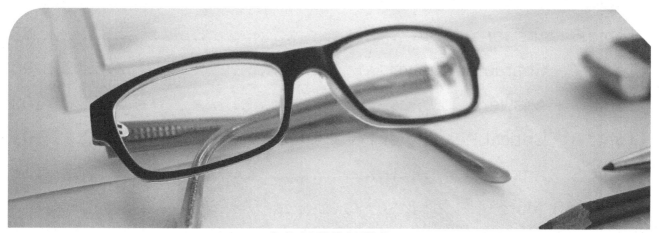

CONTENTS

ALEXANDER-GRACE EDUCATION

Understanding the MAP Tests

The NWEA MAP (Measures of Academic Progress) test is an adaptive assessment that is designed to measure student growth and progress in a variety of subject areas. The test is taken by millions of students across the United States and is widely used by educators to help inform instruction and measure student outcomes. The NWEA MAP test is administered online and provides immediate feedback on student performance, allowing teachers to adjust their teaching strategies and provide targeted support to individual students.

The NWEA MAP test is unique in that it is adaptive, which means that the difficulty of the questions adjusts based on the student's responses. This allows the test to be more personalized to each student's abilities and provides a more accurate measure of their knowledge and skills. The test covers a range of subject areas, including mathematics, reading, language usage, and science, and is administered multiple times throughout the school year. This allows teachers to track student progress and growth over time and make data-driven decisions to improve student outcomes.

Purpose and Benefits of MAP Testing

The primary purpose of the MAP Test is to provide valuable insights into a student's learning and academic progress. By offering a detailed analysis of a student's performance in reading, language usage, mathematics, and science, the test helps teachers tailor their instruction to meet individual needs. The MAP Test also serves as a benchmarking tool, allowing schools and districts to compare their students' performance with national norms and other local institutions.

This data-driven approach enables educators to make informed decisions about curriculum, instructional methods, and resource allocation, ultimately leading to improved student outcomes. Additionally, the MAP Test can help identify gifted students who may benefit from advanced or accelerated programs, as well as students who may require additional support or interventions.

Test Format and Content

The MAP Test is divided into four primary content areas: reading, language usage, mathematics, and science. Each section consists of multiple-choice questions that cover various topics and skills within the respective subject. The test is untimed, allowing students to work at their own pace and ensuring a lower level of test anxiety. The computer-adaptive nature of the MAP Test ensures that the difficulty of questions adjusts based on a student's performance, making it suitable for students of all ability levels. As a result, the MAP Test not only evaluates a student's mastery of grade-level content but also assesses their readiness for more advanced material.

Adaptive Testing and Scoring System

One of the unique aspects of the MAP Test is its adaptive testing system. As students answer questions, the test adjusts the difficulty of subsequent questions based on their performance. This adaptive nature allows the test to home in on a student's true ability level, providing more accurate and meaningful results. The MAP Test uses a RIT (Rasch Unit) scale to measure student achievement, which is an equal-interval scale that allows for easy comparison of scores across grade levels and subjects. This scoring system allows educators and parents to track a student's growth over time, making it an invaluable tool for understanding academic progress and setting individualized learning goals.

Preparing for Success on the MAP Test

Effective preparation for the MAP Test involves a combination of understanding the test format, mastering content knowledge, and developing test-taking strategies. This test prep book is designed to provide students with comprehensive guidance on each content area, offering targeted instruction and practice questions to build confidence and ensure success. Additionally, the book includes test-taking tips and strategies to help students approach the test with a calm and focused mindset. By working through this book and dedicating time to consistent practice, students will be well-equipped to excel on the MAP Test and achieve their academic goals.

Note that, since there is no cap to the level that a student can work to in preparation for this test, there is no 'completion' of content, as students can simply do questions from grades above in preparation. It should be noted that students are not expected to work far above grade level to succeed in this test, as consistent correct answers are more relevant.

ALEXANDER-GRACE EDUCATION

What Is Contained Within this Book?

Within this book you will find 320 questions based off content which would be found within the MAP test your student will take. The content found in this book will be the equivalent of grade 8 level. Note that since this test is adaptive, some students may benefit by looking at several grade levels of content, not just their own.

At the end of the book will contain answers alongside explanations. It is recommended to look and check your answers thoroughly in regular intervals to make sure you improve as similar questions come up.

Topic 1 - Interpreting Figurative Language

Once upon a time, in a land filled with rolling hills and endless skies, there lived a wise old owl named Oliver. Oliver had seen many seasons come and go, and his wisdom was as vast as the ocean. The other animals would often seek his advice, for Oliver's words were like a lighthouse guiding ships to shore. His home was in an ancient tree, which stood as a testament to history, its roots deeply intertwined with the earth's secrets. Oliver's stories were not just tales, but lessons wrapped in the cloak of night, each a beacon of light in the darkness, helping the forest dwellers navigate the journey of life.

1.1) What does Oliver the owl symbolize in the story?

☐ Wisdom and guidance

☐ Fear and darkness

☐ Youth and inexperience

☐ Loneliness and isolation

1.2) The 'lighthouse guiding ships to shore' is a metaphor for Oliver's:

☐ Mysterious past

☐ Light-hearted nature

☐ Ability to solve problems

☐ Isolation from the others

1.3) How is the ancient tree described in the story significant?

☐ As a source of food

☐ As a barrier to the outside world

☐ As a place of danger

☐ As a marker of time and history

1.4) What do Oliver's stories represent?

☐ Lessons about life

☐ Secrets of the ancient tree

☐ The history of the hills

☐ Entertainment for the forest

1.5) The phrase 'beacon of light in the darkness' suggests that Oliver's advice:

☐ Creates more questions than answers

☐ Is often ignored

☐ Serves as hope and guidance

☐ Is only useful at night

Beneath the canopy of a dense jungle, there flowed a river as clear as glass, mirroring the world above it. This river, named Whisper, had the power to reflect not just the physical beauty of the jungle, but the hearts and thoughts of those who gazed into its waters. A young panther, curious and agile, named Shadow, often visited the river to ponder the mysteries of life. The river's gentle flow and the vibrant life it nurtured were like a dance of light and shadows, revealing the delicate balance of nature. Shadow's journey alongside Whisper became a quest for understanding, a silent conversation between the spirit of the jungle and its fearless explorer.

1.6) What does the river Whisper symbolize in the story?

☐ A path of danger

☐ A source of food

☐ The mirror of truth

☐ An obstacle to overcome

1.7) Shadow's reflections by the river suggest:

☐ A journey of self-discovery

☐ A search for adventure

☐ A desire for companionship

☐ A struggle for survival

1.8) The 'dance of light and shadows' primarily illustrates:

☐ The dangers lurking in the jungle

☐ The beauty of the river

☐ The contrast between day and night

☐ The cycle of life in the jungle

1.9) How does the story portray the relationship between Shadow and Whisper?

☐ As friends

☐ As adversaries

☐ As indifferent entities

☐ As teacher and student

1.10) The story's description of the jungle's life around the river is intended to:

☐ Narrate the history of the jungle

☐ Showcase the jungle's biodiversity

☐ Highlight the isolation of the jungle

☐ Emphasize the dangers of the wild

In the quiet town of Willow Creek, every evening brought a spectacle of colors as the sky painted itself with hues of orange, pink, and purple. This daily masterpiece was the town's pride, known far and wide as the Canvas of the Gods. An old painter, Mr. Alcott, spent his life trying to capture this beauty on his canvas, believing that within this kaleidoscope of colors lay the emotions of the universe. His gallery, a small cottage at the edge of town, became a sanctuary for those seeking to understand the language of the skies. Mr. Alcott's paintings were more than art; they were windows to the soul, inviting onlookers to explore the depths of their own emotions through the strokes of his brush.

1.11) What does the 'Canvas of the Gods' symbolize in the story?

□ A hidden treasure

□ A challenge to be overcome

□ The town's isolation

□ The power of nature

1.12) Mr. Alcott's attempt to capture the evening sky on canvas represents his:

□ Conflict with the townsfolk

□ Struggle with loneliness

□ Desire to share beauty

□ Quest for perfection

1.13) The gallery is portrayed as a sanctuary because it:

□ Offers shelter from the weather

□ Allows visitors to explore their emotions

□ Provides a meeting place for artists

□ Houses valuable artifacts

1.14) Mr. Alcott's paintings are described as 'windows to the soul' because they:

☐ Capture the essence of the evening skies

☐ Reflect the viewers' inner feelings

☐ Reveal the secrets of the universe

☐ Display the beauty of Willow Creek

1.15) The story's description of the evening sky's colors primarily serves to:

☐ Convey the emotions of the universe

☐ Emphasize the town's uniqueness

☐ Set the scene for a festival

☐ Illustrate the changing seasons

Far beyond the bustling cities and the rolling hills, at the edge of the world, there was a lighthouse that guarded the coast against the relentless sea. This lighthouse, known to all as the Sentinel, was not just a beacon for ships but a symbol of hope for the weary and a guide in the darkness. The keeper of the Sentinel, an old sailor named Captain Elliott, had stories that intertwined with the sea's whispers, tales of bravery, loss, and the eternal dance between the sea and sky. His life, much like the lighthouse, was a testament to the strength and perseverance needed to face the storms, both literal and metaphorical, that life brings.

1.16) What does the Sentinel symbolize in the story?

☐ Hope and guidance

☐ Isolation and loneliness

☐ Mystery and the unknown

☐ Danger and fear

1.17) Captain Elliott's stories are most closely associated with:

☐ Life's challenges

☐ The beauty of the coast

☐ The sea's dangers

☐ Historical events

1.18) The 'eternal dance between the sea and sky' metaphorically represents:

☐ Human emotions

☐ The cycle of life

☐ The passage of time

☐ The changing weather

1.19) How is the lighthouse portrayed in relation to the sea?

☐ As a conqueror

☐ As an observer

☐ As a victim

☐ As a protector

1.20) The story's emphasis on Captain Elliott's perseverance primarily serves to:

☐ Inspire resilience in adversity

☐ Showcase his knowledge of the sea

☐ Illustrate his physical strength

☐ Highlight his solitude

In a small village nestled among towering mountains, there was a garden known for its magical blooms. This garden, curated by an enigmatic gardener named Lila, was a mosaic of colors and scents, where each flower whispered secrets of ancient magic. It was said that Lila could speak to the flowers, understanding their language as they shared the wisdom of the earth. The villagers believed that the garden was a bridge between the mundane and the mystical, a place where the veil between worlds was thinnest. Lila's garden was not just a haven for plants, but a sanctuary for souls seeking solace and connection with nature's profound mysteries.

1.21) What does Lila's ability to speak with flowers symbolize?

☐ Mastery over magic

☐ Isolation from society

☐ A deep connection with nature

☐ A secret power

1.22) The garden is portrayed as a bridge because it:

☐ Serves as a path to Lila's home

☐ Connects different communities

☐ Links the mundane to the mystical

☐ Represents the cycle of life and death

1.23) What do the 'whispers of the flowers' in the garden represent?

☐ Gossip among the villagers

☐ Directions for finding treasure

☐ Secrets of ancient magic

☐ The gardener's imagination

1.24) How does the story depict the garden in relation to the village?

☐ As a center of commerce

☐ As a sanctuary for solace

☐ As a source of envy

□ As a symbol of division

1.25) The description of the garden's blooms as 'magical' primarily serves to:

□ Emphasize their unique beauty

□ Highlight the biodiversity of the village

□ Illustrate the garden's impact on visitors

□ Suggest Lila's supernatural abilities

At the edge of the known world, where the sky meets the sea, there was a tower that reached towards the heavens. This tower, built from the dreams of those who dared to imagine, was a beacon of inspiration for all. It was said that on clear nights, one could see the light from the tower's pinnacle, a solitary star guiding the way to the realm of possibilities. The keeper of the tower, a dreamer named Elian, spent his nights gazing at the stars, weaving tales of distant worlds and adventures yet to be. Elian's stories were not mere fiction; they were invitations to believe in the boundless potential of the human spirit, a reminder that even the most distant dreams could one day be within reach.

1.26) What does the tower represent in the story?

□ A monument to the past

□ A symbol of hope and inspiration

□ A challenge to overcome

□ A barrier between worlds

1.27) Elian's role as the keeper of the tower highlights his:

□ Curiosity and imagination

□ Loneliness and isolation

□ Fear of the unknown

□ Desire for power

1.28) The 'solitary star guiding the way' is a metaphor for:

☐ Guidance towards one's dreams

☐ Individual ambition

☐ The light from the tower

☐ The pursuit of knowledge

1.29) How do Elian's stories affect those who hear them?

☐ They entertain without deeper impact

☐ They instill a sense of fear

☐ They cause confusion

☐ They inspire belief in potential

1.30) The description of the tower 'reaching towards the heavens' serves to:

☐ Compare it to natural wonders

☐ Emphasize its architectural grandeur

☐ Showcase its visibility from afar

☐ Illustrate the aspiration to achieve the impossible

In the midst of a vast desert, where the sun painted the sand with gold and the nights unveiled a tapestry of stars, there lay an oasis, a jewel of life amidst the arid expanse. This oasis, known as Mirage, was no ordinary haven; it was believed to be a gift from the heavens, a place where the weary could find solace and the thirsty could quench their parched souls. The guardian of Mirage, a wise and gentle spirit named Zara, was said to have the ability to speak with the wind and listen to the sand, understanding the ancient tales they whispered. Zara's presence made the oasis not just a refuge for travelers, but a sanctuary where one could learn the secrets of the desert, uncover the mysteries of life, and perhaps discover the true meaning of oasis.

1.31) What does the oasis represent in the story?

☐ A gateway to another world

☐ A place of danger and deceit

☐ A source of wealth

☐ A symbol of hope and survival

1.32) Zara's ability to communicate with the wind and sand suggests:

☐ A deep connection with the desert

☐ Loneliness and desire for company

☐ Magical powers over nature

☐ Control over the elements

1.33) The 'tapestry of stars' seen at night symbolizes:

☐ The beauty of the universe

☐ The secrets of the desert

☐ The dreams of the travelers

☐ Guidance for the lost

1.34) How is Mirage different from the surrounding desert?

☐ It is a mirage and not real

☐ It is more dangerous

☐ It offers life and refuge

☐ It hides valuable treasures

1.35) The story's depiction of Zara primarily serves to:

☐ Emphasize the power of nature

☐ Illustrate the importance of guardianship

☐ Highlight the wisdom found in solitude

☐ Introduce a mythical character

In the heart of an ancient forest, where trees whispered secrets of the old world and the air was thick with enchantment, there stood a library carved out of the very essence of magic itself. This library, known as the Archive of Echoes, was guarded by a keeper named Elinor, who was as timeless as the tales within its walls. The Archive was not just a collection of books; it was a repository of dreams, a place where every volume held a different universe, waiting to be discovered. Visitors to the Archive could hear the echoes of a thousand stories, each one a thread in the tapestry of the cosmos. Elinor's task was to guide seekers on their journey through the pages, helping them to find the stories that resonated with their souls, teaching them that every echo was a key to unlocking their own story.

1.36) What does the Archive of Echoes represent in the story?

☐ A treasure to be taken

☐ A hidden danger in the forest

☐ A place of knowledge and discovery

☐ A lost civilization

1.37) Elinor's role as the keeper of the Archive emphasizes her:

☐ Power and control

☐ Wisdom and guidance

☐ Curiosity and adventure

☐ Loneliness and sorrow

1.38) The 'repository of dreams' metaphor suggests the Archive is:

☐ A center for magical research

☐ A collection of stories and possibilities

☐ A museum of ancient artifacts

☐ A place where visitors can sleep

1.39) How does the story convey the importance of the books in the Archive?

☐ Through their protective enchantments

☐ By describing them as gateways to universes

☐ Through the magical powers they grant

☐ By highlighting their age and rarity

1.40) The concept of 'echoes' in the story is used to illustrate:

☐ The haunting presence of the past

☐ The connection between stories and personal identity

☐ The sounds of the forest

☐ The repetition of history

Topic 1 - Answers

Question Number	Answer	Explanation
1.1	Wisdom and guidance	Oliver symbolizes wisdom and guidance, acting as a mentor to other animals.
1.2	Ability to solve problems	The metaphor suggests Oliver's advice helps others navigate their issues, similar to a lighthouse guiding ships.
1.3	As a marker of time and history	The ancient tree signifies the passage of time and history, emphasizing the depth of Oliver's wisdom.
1.4	Lessons about life	Oliver's stories are metaphorical lessons on life, offering guidance and wisdom.
1.5	Serves as hope and guidance	Oliver's advice acts as a source of hope and direction for others in dark times.
1.6	The mirror of truth	Whisper symbolizes reflection, both literal and metaphorical, revealing truths to those who look into it.
1.7	A journey of self-discovery	Shadow's reflections by the river suggest a personal quest for understanding and insight.
1.8	The beauty of the river	The phrase illustrates the harmony and beauty of life around Whisper, emphasizing the balance of nature.
1.9	As teacher and student	The story portrays Whisper and Shadow's relationship as one of mutual learning and exploration.
1.10	Showcase the jungle's biodiversity	The vibrant life nurtured by Whisper highlights the jungle's rich biodiversity and the balance of nature.
1.11	The power of nature	The Canvas of the Gods symbolizes the overwhelming and awe-inspiring power of the natural world.
1.12	Desire to share beauty	Mr. Alcott's efforts to capture the sky's beauty on canvas represent his wish to share this splendor with others.
1.13	Allows visitors to explore their emotions	The gallery serves as a sanctuary where visitors can connect with their feelings through art.
1.14	Reflect the viewers' inner feelings	The paintings act as mirrors, enabling viewers to see and explore their emotions.
1.15	Convey the emotions of the universe	The vivid description of the sky's colors serves to express the vast range of emotions contained within the universe.
1.16	Hope and guidance	The Sentinel symbolizes hope and guidance, offering direction and comfort to those at sea.
1.17	Life's challenges	Captain Elliott's stories relate to the challenges of life, paralleling the struggles faced by sailors and the broader human experience.
1.18	The cycle of life	The metaphor signifies the ongoing cycle of life and nature, reflected in the interactions between the sea and sky.

1.19	As a protector	The lighthouse is portrayed as a guardian against the dangers of the sea, providing safety and direction.
1.20	Inspire resilience in adversity	Captain Elliott's perseverance through storms symbolizes the strength needed to face life's challenges.
1.21	A deep connection with nature	Lila's ability to communicate with flowers indicates a profound bond with the natural world, transcending human understanding.
1.22	Links the mundane to the mystical	The garden acts as a conduit between the everyday world and the mystical, revealing the hidden magic of nature.
1.23	Secrets of ancient magic	The whispers of the flowers suggest that the garden holds ancient magical knowledge, shared with Lila.
1.24	As a sanctuary for solace	The garden provides a peaceful retreat for those seeking comfort and a deeper connection with nature.
1.25	Emphasize their unique beauty	Describing the blooms as 'magical' highlights their extraordinary beauty and the garden's mystical qualities.
1.26	A symbol of hope and inspiration	The tower stands as a beacon of hope and creativity, encouraging others to dream and aspire.
1.27	Curiosity and imagination	Elian's role emphasizes his imaginative spirit and quest for knowledge, reflected in his storytelling.
1.28	Guidance towards one's dreams	The metaphor suggests that just like the star guides travelers, the tower inspires individuals to follow their dreams.
1.29	They inspire belief in potential	Elian's stories encourage others to believe in their capabilities and the possibility of achieving their dreams.
1.30	Illustrate the aspiration to achieve the impossible	The tower reaching for the heavens symbolizes the human desire to pursue lofty goals and the boundless nature of human ambition.
1.31	A symbol of hope and survival	The oasis represents a vital source of life and hope in the harsh desert environment, offering refuge and sustenance.
1.32	A deep connection with the desert	Zara's ability to understand the desert's elements suggests an intimate bond with the natural world, embodying its essence.
1.33	The beauty of the universe	The nighttime sky over the oasis symbolizes the vast, mysterious beauty of the universe and the wonder it inspires.
1.34	It offers life and refuge	Mirage stands in contrast to the barren desert as a life-giving haven, supporting both the physical and spiritual needs of travelers.
1.35	Illustrate the importance of guardianship	Zara's guardianship of the oasis emphasizes the role of protectors in preserving and interpreting the natural world's mysteries.
1.36	A place of knowledge and discovery	The Archive of Echoes serves as a hub of wisdom and exploration, where seekers can discover vast universes within books.
1.37	Wisdom and guidance	Elinor's guardianship of the Archive signifies her role as a guide, helping visitors navigate the depths of knowledge and self-discovery.
1.38	A collection of stories and possibilities	Describing the Archive as a 'repository of dreams' highlights its role as a source of infinite stories and potential discoveries.
1.39	By describing them as gateways to universes	The books in the Archive are portrayed as portals to other worlds, emphasizing the transformative power of reading.
1.40	The connection between stories and personal identity	The concept of 'echoes' suggests that stories reflect and influence personal identities, shaping individuals' narratives.

Topic 2 – Analyzing Literary Techniques

In the small, seemingly peaceful town of Greenwood, an unexpected event was about to unfold. Mrs. Thompson, the town's beloved librarian, discovered a mysterious book hidden behind other volumes on a dusty shelf. The book, bound in faded leather, contained stories of the town's history that no one remembered. As she turned the pages, she realized that the events described eerily predicted current happenings in Greenwood. Unbeknownst to her, this discovery would soon unravel the fabric of the town's reality, revealing secrets that had been hidden for decades. The book was not just a collection of tales; it was a mirror reflecting the truth through the shadows of the past.

2.1) What literary technique is used to hint at future events in Greenwood?

☐ Flashback

☐ Metaphor

☐ Irony

☐ Foreshadowing

2.2) How does the discovery of the mysterious book contribute to the narrative?

☐ It introduces a flashback

☐ It creates a subplot

☐ It provides comic relief

☐ It serves as a turning point

2.3) The use of the mysterious book to reveal the town's secrets is an example of:

☐ Personification

☐ Symbolism

☐ Irony

☐ Alliteration

2.4) Which technique describes the story's reflection of truth through past events?

☐ Hyperbole

☐ Flashback

☐ Allusion

☐ Foreshadowing

2.5) Mrs. Thompson's unawareness of the book's significance can be seen as:

☐ Dramatic irony

☐ Situational irony

☐ Satire

☐ Verbal irony

Evan stood at the edge of the cliff, looking out over the sea, reflecting on his journey. Just a week ago, he had found an old map in his grandfather's attic, marking a path to a hidden treasure. Each step of his adventure seemed to be guided by fate, as if the map was not just leading him to treasure, but also to a deeper understanding of his family's legacy. The night before his discovery, he had dreamt of the sea, a foreshadowing that now felt eerily prescient. Little did he know, the greatest treasure he would find at journey's end was not gold or jewels, but the revelation of his grandfather's heroism during a long-forgotten sea voyage.

2.6) Evan's dream of the sea the night before finding the map is an example of:

☐ Metaphor

☐ Foreshadowing

☐ Irony

☐ Simile

2.7) The map leading Evan to understand his family's legacy is a form of:

☐ Alliteration

☐ Flashback

☐ Hyperbole

☐ Symbolism

2.8) Which literary technique is used to reveal the grandfather's heroism?

☐ Irony

☐ Personification

☐ Flashback

☐ Onomatopoeia

2.9) The treasure at journey's end symbolizing a personal revelation is an example of:

☐ Situational irony

☐ Verbal irony

☐ Allegory

☐ Metaphor

2.10) Evan's realization about his grandfather's heroism can be considered:

☐ An epilogue

☐ A prologue

☐ An antagonist

☐ A climax

Under the glow of a full moon, Lily ventured into the ancient forest that bordered her village, drawn by tales of a mysterious figure who granted wishes to the brave of heart. The forest, alive with whispers of the past, seemed to guide her steps towards an old, ivy-covered well said to be the dwelling of the wish-granter. As she approached, she recalled her grandmother's stories, which had always seemed like fairy tales, but now felt like memories awakening. Upon reaching the well, Lily whispered her wish into the darkness below. The response came not in words, but as a glimpse of her future, revealing the impact of her wish in a vision that was both a warning and a promise.

2.11) The ancient forest serving as a guide to Lily is an example of:

☐ Personification

☐ Onomatopoeia

☐ Simile

☐ Metaphor

2.12) Lily's recollection of her grandmother's stories as she approaches the well illustrates:

☐ Irony

☐ Foreshadowing

☐ Hyperbole

☐ Flashback

2.13) The vision Lily receives can be interpreted as a form of:

☐ Metonymy

☐ Symbolism

☐ Allegory

☐ Irony

2.14) The mysterious figure who grants wishes is used to introduce:

☐ A resolution

☐ A plot twist

☐ A climax

☐ A conflict

2.15) How does the story use the full moon in the narrative?

☐ As a symbol of fear

☐ To set the mood

☐ To foreshadow events

☐ As a time marker

The clock struck midnight as Alex found himself standing before the old mansion at the end of Willow Lane. Legend had it that every century, on the night of the blue moon, the mansion's true owner, a ghost from the 18th century, would appear to reclaim his home. Alex, a skeptic, wanted to debunk the myth but felt an inexplicable chill as the air around him grew denser. Suddenly, the door creaked open, revealing not a ghost, but a room filled with mirrors showing not reflections, but scenes from the past. Each mirror was a portal to a moment in history, challenging Alex's disbelief and offering a chance to witness the stories he had only read about in books.

2.16) The legend of the mansion's true owner appearing is an example of:

☐ Foreshadowing

☐ Alliteration

☐ Hyperbole

☐ Irony

2.17) Alex's skepticism turning into a confrontation with the past illustrates:

☐ Character development

☐ Symbolism

☐ A moral lesson

☐ A plot twist

2.18) The mirrors showing scenes from the past serve as:

☐ A metaphor for reflection

☐ Symbolism for truth

☐ An allegory for history

☐ Hyperbole for change

2.19) How does the story use the midnight setting?

☐ To introduce new characters

☐ As a climax

☐ To symbolize hope

☐ To create suspense

2.20) The air growing denser around Alex as he approaches the mansion is used to:

☐ Introduce a subplot

☐ Describe the weather

☐ Illustrate Alex's fear

☐ Foreshadow an upcoming event

On a stormy night, with thunder echoing through the mountains, Sarah discovered an old journal in the attic of her ancestral home. The journal belonged to her great-great-grandmother, who was rumored to be a powerful witch. As Sarah flipped through the pages, she found a story that mirrored her own life, filled with similar challenges and choices. The journal described a pivotal night when her ancestor had to make a decision that would change the course of their family's history. Intrigued, Sarah read on, realizing that the storm outside was not just a coincidence but a parallel to the storm her ancestor faced, a symbolic reminder of the ongoing struggle between destiny and free will.

2.21) Sarah finding a journal that mirrors her own life is an example of:

☐ Foreshadowing

☐ Irony

☐ Symbolism

☐ Parallelism

2.22) The storm serving as a backdrop to Sarah's discovery illustrates:

☐ Foreshadowing

☐ Symbolism

☐ Metaphor

☐ Hyperbole

2.23) The concept of destiny versus free will in the story is explored through:

☐ The setting

☐ The plot

☐ The characters' dialogue

☐ Allegory

2.24) How does the story use the ancestral journal?

☐ To provide historical context

☐ To foreshadow future events

☐ As a plot device to introduce conflict

☐ As a symbol for legacy

2.25) The pivotal night described in the journal acts as:

☐ A turning point

☐ An exposition

☐ A resolution

☐ A climax

In the bustling market of the ancient city, where spices and silk wove a tapestry of colors and scents, Marco, a young apprentice, stumbled upon a curious artifact. It was a compass that pointed not north, but to one's deepest desires. Intrigued by its power, Marco decided to follow the compass, leading him through narrow alleys and hidden courtyards, each turn revealing secrets of the city and of himself. The journey was not just about the destination but about the lessons learned along the way. As Marco ventured deeper, he realized that the true discovery was not the treasure the compass sought, but the realization of his own potential and the understanding that true direction comes from within.

2.26) The compass pointing to one's deepest desires is an example of:

☐ Metaphor

☐ Irony

☐ Simile

☐ Personification

2.27) Marco's journey through the city serves as:

☐ Symbolism for wealth

☐ An allegory for self-discovery

☐ Foreshadowing of future events

☐ A flashback to his past

2.28) The story's setting in the ancient market is used to:

☐ Highlight cultural diversity

☐ Set the mood for adventure

☐ Provide historical accuracy

☐ Introduce the antagonist

2.29) Marco's realization that true direction comes from within illustrates:

☐ A resolution

☐ A climax

☐ Character development

☐ An external conflict

2.30) How does the artifact act within the story?

☐ As a symbol of power

☐ As a historical relic

☐ As a catalyst for the plot

☐ As a source of conflict

As the sun dipped below the horizon, casting long shadows over the abandoned village, Emily discovered an ancient diary tucked away in the ruins of a crumbling cottage. The diary belonged to a sorceress who had protected the village long ago, using her powers to shield it from harm. Each entry revealed the sorceress's battles, her victories, and her fears, painting a vivid picture of a time when magic was the village's last defense. Emily, feeling a connection to the sorceress, realized that the diary was not merely a record of the past but a message for the future. The final entry, dated but never completed, hinted at a spell that could revive the village, a task that now fell to Emily as she embraced her own hidden power.

2.31) The diary serving as a link between Emily and the sorceress represents:

☐ Symbolism

☐ Hyperbole

☐ Metaphor

☐ Irony

2.32) The setting sun casting long shadows over the village primarily symbolizes:

☐ A new beginning

☐ The end of an era

☐ The approach of danger

☐ The passage of time

2.33) Emily's realization about the diary's purpose illustrates:

☐ A turning point in the plot

☐ Character development

☐ Foreshadowing

☐ An internal conflict

2.34) The unfinished entry about a revival spell suggests:

☐ An unresolved conflict

☐ A cliffhanger

☐ Foreshadowing of Emily's journey

☐ Symbolism for hope

2.35) How does the story convey the theme of embracing one's destiny?

☐ With the description of the sorceress's battles

☐ Through the diary's historical entries

☐ By illustrating the village's abandonment

☐ Through Emily's acceptance of her power

In the heart of a dense forest, where light barely touched the ground, there was a hidden glen known to few. This glen, bathed in a perpetual twilight, was home to the Whispering Trees, ancient beings that could communicate with those who listened closely. Kai, a young explorer with a keen sense for the unusual, ventured into this forest, drawn by tales of its mysteries. As he approached the glen, the trees began to murmur, each whisper revealing secrets of the forest's past and visions of its future. Kai realized that the forest was not just a place of mystery, but a guardian of wisdom, offering insights to those brave enough to seek them. The whispers, though cryptic, guided Kai to a newfound understanding of his place in the world, intertwining his destiny with that of the forest itself.

2.36) The Whispering Trees in the story are an example of:

☐ Irony

☐ Metaphor

☐ Simile

☐ Personification

2.37) Kai being drawn to the forest by tales of its mysteries illustrates:

□ Allegory

□ Foreshadowing

□ Irony

□ Symbolism

2.38) The glen being bathed in perpetual twilight primarily symbolizes:

□ The unknown

□ Danger lurking

□ Eternal peace

□ A threshold between worlds

2.39) The whispers guiding Kai to an understanding of his place in the world represent:

□ Symbolism

□ A moral lesson

□ Character development

□ A climax

2.40) How does the story use the concept of destiny intertwining with the forest?

□ As a plot twist

□ As a setting description

□ To introduce a new character

□ To illustrate the theme of interconnectedness

Topic 2 - Answers

Question Number	Answer	Explanation
2.1	Foreshadowing	The story hints at future events in Greenwood through the use of foreshadowing, suggesting a connection between the book's tales and current happenings.
2.2	It serves as a turning point	The discovery of the mysterious book changes the course of the narrative, revealing the town's hidden secrets.
2.3	Symbolism	The mysterious book symbolizes the reflection of truth, revealing the town's hidden past through its stories.
2.4	Foreshadowing	The reflection of truth through past events is achieved using foreshadowing, hinting at the impact of these events on the present.
2.5	Dramatic irony	Mrs. Thompson's unawareness of the book's significance, while the reader understands its importance, is an example of dramatic irony.
2.6	Foreshadowing	Evan's dream about the sea before finding the map serves as foreshadowing, hinting at the significance of his upcoming journey.
2.7	Symbolism	The map symbolizes Evan's journey to understanding his family's legacy, representing a deeper exploration of his heritage.
2.8	Flashback	The revelation of the grandfather's heroism is likely shared through a flashback, revealing his past actions and their significance.
2.9	Allegory	The treasure symbolizing a personal revelation can be seen as an allegory, representing Evan's discovery of his grandfather's heroism and its impact on his own identity.
2.10	A climax	Evan's realization about his grandfather's heroism represents the climax of his journey, marking a significant moment of discovery and understanding.
2.11	Personification	The ancient forest guiding Lily is personified, suggesting that it has a will or consciousness that helps her find her way.
2.12	Flashback	Lily recalling her grandmother's stories as memories awakening suggests the use of flashback to connect past tales with her current experience.
2.13	Symbolism	The vision received at the well symbolizes foresight and potential consequences, serving as a symbolic message about the impact of Lily's wish.
2.14	A conflict	The introduction of the mysterious figure who grants wishes sets up a conflict, presenting Lily with a challenge or decision to make.
2.15	To set the mood	The full moon is used to set a mystical or eerie mood for Lily's adventure, enhancing the story's atmosphere.
2.16	Foreshadowing	The legend of the mansion's true owner is an example of foreshadowing, hinting at the ghostly appearance and the night's mysterious events.
2.17	A plot twist	Alex's skepticism leading to a confrontation with historical scenes instead of a ghost introduces a plot twist, challenging his disbelief.
2.18	Symbolism for truth	The mirrors showing scenes from the past symbolize a deeper truth about history and the mansion, revealing hidden stories.
2.19	To create suspense	The midnight setting is used to create suspense, setting up a tense atmosphere for the supernatural encounter.

2.20	Foreshadow an upcoming event	The air growing denser is used to foreshadow the supernatural experience Alex is about to have, building anticipation.
2.21	Parallelism	The journal mirroring Sarah's life is an example of parallelism, drawing a direct comparison between their experiences.
2.22	Symbolism	The storm symbolizes turmoil and change, paralleling the internal and historical struggles described in the journal.
2.23	Allegory	The story explores destiny versus free will through allegory, using the storm and journal as metaphors for life's choices.
2.24	As a symbol for legacy	The ancestral journal is used as a symbol for legacy, connecting Sarah to her past and the choices that shaped her family.
2.25	A turning point	The pivotal night described acts as a turning point, highlighting a moment of significant decision or change.
2.26	Metaphor	The compass is a metaphor for personal desires and the pursuit of what one truly seeks, guiding Marco beyond geographical directions.
2.27	An allegory for self-discovery	Marco's journey, guided by the compass, serves as an allegory for self-discovery, exploring internal landscapes and personal growth.
2.28	Set the mood for adventure	The ancient market setting establishes the mood for adventure, immersing Marco and the reader in a world of exploration and mystery.
2.29	Character development	Marco's realization represents his character development, as he understands that true direction and fulfillment come from within.
2.30	As a catalyst for the plot	The curious artifact, the compass, acts as a catalyst for the plot, propelling Marco on his journey of discovery and self-realization.
2.31	Symbolism	The diary linking Emily to the sorceress symbolizes a connection across time, embodying the continuity of power and legacy.
2.32	The passage of time	The setting sun and long shadows symbolize the passage of time, reflecting on the village's history and its current state of abandonment.
2.33	Character development	Emily's realization about the diary's purpose illustrates her character development, as she begins to understand her role in the village's fate.
2.34	Foreshadowing of Emily's journey	The unfinished entry about a revival spell foreshadows Emily's involvement in the village's restoration, hinting at her future actions.
2.35	Through Emily's acceptance of her power	The theme of embracing one's destiny is conveyed through Emily's acceptance of her hidden power, recognizing her role in continuing her ancestor's legacy.
2.36	Personification	The Whispering Trees are personified, attributed with the ability to communicate, symbolizing a deep connection between nature and humanity.
2.37	Foreshadowing	Kai being drawn to the forest by tales of its mysteries serves as foreshadowing, hinting at the discoveries and transformations he will experience.
2.38	A threshold between worlds	The perpetual twilight symbolizes a liminal space, suggesting the glen is a threshold between the known world and the mystical.
2.39	Symbolism	The whispers guiding Kai symbolize the wisdom of nature, offering insights that lead to personal growth and understanding.
2.40	To illustrate the theme of interconnectedness	The intertwining of Kai's destiny with the forest illustrates the theme of interconnectedness, highlighting the bond between individuals and their environment.

Topic 3 – Understanding Author's Craft

In the quaint town of Penfield, where every street corner had a story, lived an author named Ms. Clara. Her writing, known for its vivid imagery and sharp wit, captured the essence of Penfield's charm. Ms. Clara's latest novel, 'The Whispering Winds of Penfield,' was a masterpiece of satire and paradox, reflecting the town's peculiarities with a humorous yet poignant tone. Through her unique voice, she navigated the complexities of small-town life, weaving tales that resonated with both the young and the old. Her ability to craft characters that were both relatable and extraordinarily unique made her stories a beacon of light in the literary world of Penfield.

3.1) Ms. Clara's use of satire in her novel primarily serves to:

☐ Criticize societal norms

☐ Create suspenseful plots

☐ Develop complex characters

☐ Describe the setting in detail

3.2) The tone of 'The Whispering Winds of Penfield' can best be described as:

☐ Humorous yet poignant

☐ Detached and objective

☐ Optimistic and uplifting

☐ Solemn and serious

3.3) Ms. Clara's unique voice in her writing is characterized by:

☐ Vivid imagery and sharp wit

☐ Lengthy descriptions of nature

☐ Simplistic language and themes

☐ Predictable storylines

3.4) How does Ms. Clara navigate the complexities of small-town life in her stories?

☐ By focusing on international events

☐ Through tales that resonate with all ages

☐ By ignoring the flaws of the town

☐ Using a single perspective for all characters

3.5) The paradox in 'The Whispering Winds of Penfield' is used to:

☐ Contrast characters' desires with reality

☐ Introduce new characters

☐ Outline the history of Penfield

☐ Provide a detailed map of the town

Oliver, a renowned poet from the coastal town of Seaview, had a knack for capturing the essence of the sea in his verses. His latest collection, 'Echoes of the Tide,' was a blend of metaphor and alliteration, bringing to life the rhythmic dance of the waves and the timeless tales of the deep. Oliver's voice, both gentle and powerful, invited readers to look beyond the surface, exploring themes of change and resilience. With each poem, he utilized a distinct tone that mirrored the sea's many moods, from the serene whispers of dawn to the tempestuous roars of a storm. Through 'Echoes of the Tide,' Oliver demonstrated his mastery of language, creating a tapestry of imagery that left readers feeling as though they had walked along the shores of Seaview themselves.

3.6) Oliver's use of metaphor in 'Echoes of the Tide' primarily serves to:

☐ Provide technical information about tides

☐ Illustrate the sea's power and beauty

☐ Describe the physical appearance of the sea

☐ Detail the history of Seaview

3.7) The collection's tone changes to reflect the sea's moods, demonstrating Oliver's skill in:

□ Setting description

□ Voice modulation

□ Character development

□ Plot structuring

3.8) 'Echoes of the Tide' employs alliteration to:

□ Introduce new characters

□ Argue against ocean pollution

□ Outline the plot of each poem

□ Emphasize the rhythmic quality of the sea

3.9) How does Oliver invite readers to explore themes of change and resilience?

□ By focusing solely on the sea's tranquility

□ Through vivid imagery and thematic depth

□ Through detailed biographies of sailors

□ By using a consistent tone throughout

3.10) The imagery in Oliver's poetry makes readers feel as if they have:

□ Met Oliver in person

□ Learned about marine biology

□ Understood complex poetic forms

□ Visited Seaview's shores

In the bustling city of Lumina, where neon lights clashed with the stars, Jenna penned her novel under the cloak of night. Her narrative wove through the lives of characters who danced on the edge of light and shadow, embodying the paradoxes of the city itself. Jenna's style, marked by concise dialogue and vivid descriptions, painted a picture of Lumina that was both gritty and enchanting. Through irony and paradox, she explored the themes of identity and belonging, challenging readers to see beyond the facade of urban life. Her novel, 'Shadows of Lumina,' became a mirror to the souls of its readers, reflecting the light and darkness within.

3.11) Jenna's exploration of identity and belonging in 'Shadows of Lumina' uses which literary device?

☐ Onomatopoeia

☐ Satire

☐ Irony

☐ Alliteration

3.12) The setting of Lumina is portrayed through:

☐ Technical jargon

☐ Simplistic language

☐ Extensive monologues

☐ Concise dialogue and vivid descriptions

3.13) How does 'Shadows of Lumina' challenge readers?

☐ Requiring knowledge of Lumina's history

☐ By offering complex puzzles

☐ Through its unconventional structure

☐ Asking them to see beyond urban life's facade

3.14) The paradoxes of the city reflected in the characters illustrate:

☐ A thematic depth

☐ Character development

☐ A narrative technique

☐ A plot twist

3.15) 'Shadows of Lumina' becoming a mirror to the souls of its readers implies that the novel:

☐ Reflects personal struggles and triumphs

☐ Focuses on supernatural elements

☐ Is primarily autobiographical

☐ Is difficult to understand

The small village of Eldridge was known for its annual festival of lights, a tradition that illuminated the night and brought together the hearts of all its residents. This year, however, the festival was the backdrop for Theo's novel, 'The Luminous Heart of Eldridge.' In his book, Theo employed a lyrical style, blending poetry with prose to capture the ethereal beauty of the festival. His narrative voice was both nostalgic and hopeful, reflecting the dual nature of the event: a celebration of light amidst the darkness. Through the use of satire, Theo also critiqued the commercialization of traditional celebrations, weaving a tale that was as thought-provoking as it was visually stunning.

3.16) Theo's lyrical style in 'The Luminous Heart of Eldridge' is characterized by:

☐ Employing a detached tone

☐ Using technical jargon

☐ Focusing on action-driven narrative

☐ Blending poetry with prose

3.17) What narrative voice does Theo use in his novel?

□ Objective and factual

□ Humorous and irreverent

□ Nostalgic and hopeful

□ Pessimistic and cynical

3.18) The use of satire in Theo's novel serves to critique:

□ The complexity of character relationships

□ The commercialization of traditional celebrations

□ The accuracy of historical events

□ The description of the village's geography

3.19) 'The Luminous Heart of Eldridge' reflects the dual nature of the festival as:

□ An event of joy and sorrow

□ A celebration of light amidst darkness

□ A symbol of unity and division

□ A gathering of past and future

3.20) How does Theo's novel make the festival visually stunning?

□ With maps of the village

□ By describing the festival's lights and colors

□ Using dialogue among villagers

□ Through detailed character costumes

In the heart of the bustling city of Meridian, where stories unfolded at every corner, Layla found her muse among the shadows and light of the urban landscape. Her graphic novel, 'Meridian: City of Shadows,' utilized stark contrasts and dynamic panel layouts to tell the tales of its inhabitants. Layla's craft was evident in her ability to convey emotion and narrative depth through minimalistic dialogue and expressive artwork. Her work was a study in paradox, capturing the isolation felt in a crowded city and the moments of connection in the most unexpected places. Through 'Meridian: City of Shadows,' Layla challenged her readers to find beauty in the mundane and to recognize the stories hidden in plain sight.

3.21) Layla's use of stark contrasts in her graphic novel emphasizes:

☐ The division between characters

☐ The dynamic nature of the city

☐ Differences in narrative pace

☐ Technical aspects of the artwork

3.22) The minimalistic dialogue in 'Meridian: City of Shadows' is used to:

☐ Highlight the artwork's expressiveness

☐ Simplify the plot

☐ Reduce character development

☐ Focus on the setting

3.23) 'Meridian: City of Shadows' captures the paradox of:

☐ Silence in noise

☐ Chaos in order

☐ Isolation in a crowded city

☐ Joy in solitude

3.24) Layla challenges her readers to find beauty in:

☐ Complex narratives

☐ The mundane

☐ Historical references

☐ Future possibilities

3.25) How does the graphic novel convey narrative depth?

☐ By focusing on a single character

☐ Through the use of color

☐ Using expressive artwork and minimalistic dialogue

☐ Through detailed backstories

Amidst the serene beauty of the countryside, where the hills whispered ancient secrets, Nora embarked on writing her memoir, 'Whispers of the Hills.' Her narrative was a blend of reflective prose and insightful observations, offering a window into the soul of the countryside and its influence on her life. Nora's style, characterized by a lyrical tone and the use of vivid imagery, invited readers to experience the beauty and tranquility of nature alongside her. Through her memoir, Nora explored the concept of home, not just as a place, but as a feeling deeply rooted in one's heart, shaped by the land and its stories. 'Whispers of the Hills' was more than a personal journey; it was a tribute to the timeless bond between humans and the natural world.

3.26) Nora's narrative style in 'Whispers of the Hills' can best be described as:

☐ Technical and factual

☐ Dialog-driven and fast-paced

☐ Lyrical and imagery-rich

☐ Concise and straightforward

3.27) The memoir's exploration of home emphasizes:

☐ Physical locations

☐ Architectural styles

☐ Historical events

☐ Emotional connections to the land

3.28) 'Whispers of the Hills' serves as a tribute to:

☐ Famous landmarks

☐ The history of the countryside

☐ The bond between humans and nature

☐ Nora's achievements

3.29) How does Nora invite readers into her experience of nature?

☐ Through interviews with locals

☐ By providing statistical data

☐ Through the use of vivid imagery

☐ By listing the names of plants

3.30) The concept of home in the memoir is depicted as:

☐ A community of people

☐ A specific house

☐ A feeling rooted in the heart

☐ A collection of personal belongings

In the bustling metropolis of New Haven, where the rhythm of life moved to the beat of the unseen, Aaron, a playwright, sought to capture the essence of urban existence in his latest play, 'Voices of New Haven.' His script was a mosaic of dialogues and monologues, each character a facet of the city's diverse populace. Aaron's craft lay in his ability to weave satire and dramatic irony into the fabric of his narratives, shedding light on the contradictions and challenges of city living. Through 'Voices of New Haven,' Aaron provided a platform for the unheard, turning the stage into a mirror reflecting the complexities of society, urging his audience to listen, reflect, and, above all, to understand.

3.31) Aaron's play 'Voices of New Haven' utilizes what literary devices to explore urban life?

☐ Satire and dramatic irony

☐ Flashbacks and foreshadowing

☐ Hyperbole and understatement

☐ Allegory and symbolism

3.32) The script's structure, featuring dialogues and monologues, aims to:

☐ Simplify the plot for clarity

☐ Emphasize the setting's historical significance

☐ Highlight the city's diversity

☐ Focus on a single protagonist

3.33) Through his play, Aaron aims to provide a platform for:

☐ The unheard voices of the city

☐ A critique of modern theater

☐ A history of New Haven

☐ Celebrating the city's achievements

3.34) 'Voices of New Haven' turns the stage into a mirror to reflect:

☐ The complexities of society

☐ The evolution of theatrical styles

☐ The beauty of urban architecture

☐ The personal journey of Aaron

3.35) Aaron's ability to shed light on city living's contradictions and challenges demonstrates his:

☐ Insight into human nature and society

☐ Mastery of historical research

☐ Expertise in character development

☐ Technical skill in set design

Deep within the archives of an ancient library, where secrets lay buried under layers of dust, Maya embarked on a quest to uncover a lost manuscript believed to hold the key to an age-old mystery. Her journey was not just a search for a physical document, but a voyage into the heart of storytelling itself. Maya's approach to the narrative was innovative, employing nonlinear storytelling and multiple perspectives to unravel the tale. Her writing, rich with metaphors and symbolism, invited readers to engage actively, piecing together the fragments of the story. 'The Manuscript of Ages,' Maya's novel, became a testament to the power of stories to transcend time, inviting exploration of themes such as knowledge, power, and the very nature of truth.

3.36) Maya's use of nonlinear storytelling and multiple perspectives in 'The Manuscript of Ages' serves to:

☐ Provide historical accuracy

☐ Simplify the narrative structure

☐ Focus on a single character's development

☐ Enhance the mystery and complexity

3.37) The rich use of metaphors and symbolism in Maya's writing:

☐ Limits the audience's understanding

☐ Requires readers to engage actively

☐ Clarifies the plot for readers

☐ Distracts from the main storyline

3.38) 'The Manuscript of Ages' explores themes of:

☐ Sportsmanship and competition

☐ Travel and exploration

☐ Knowledge, power, and truth

☐ Romance and adventure

3.39) Maya's novel is a testament to the power of stories to:

☐ Transcend time and invite exploration

☐ Serve as historical documents

☐ Teach moral lessons explicitly

☐ Entertain with light-hearted tales

3.40) How does Maya invite readers into the heart of storytelling?

☐ By focusing on action-packed scenes

☐ Through innovative narrative techniques

☐ By avoiding complex themes

☐ Using a straightforward chronological order

Topic 3 - Answers

Question Number	Answer	Explanation
3.1	Criticize societal norms	Ms. Clara's use of satire in her novel likely aims to critique or mock societal norms and behaviors in a humorous yet insightful way.
3.2	Humorous yet poignant	The novel's tone, being both humorous and poignant, suggests it deals with serious themes through a lens of humor, reflecting on the town's peculiarities.
3.3	Vivid imagery and sharp wit	Her unique voice in writing is characterized by vivid descriptions that bring scenes to life and sharp wit that adds humor and insight.
3.4	Through tales that resonate with all ages	Ms. Clara navigates small-town complexities by crafting stories that connect with readers of every age, suggesting a universal appeal and understanding.
3.5	Contrast characters' desires with reality	The paradox in her novel is likely used to highlight the difference between what characters wish for and their actual circumstances, enhancing the satire.
3.6	Illustrate the sea's power and beauty	Oliver uses metaphor in his poetry to evoke the sea's majesty and its influential presence, making abstract concepts more tangible and relatable.
3.7	Voice modulation	The collection's tone changes reflect Oliver's ability to adapt his narrative voice to match the sea's varying moods, showcasing his linguistic skill.
3.8	Emphasize the rhythmic quality of the sea	Alliteration is employed to mimic the sea's rhythm and flow, enhancing the lyrical quality of the poetry and engaging the reader's auditory imagination.
3.9	Through vivid imagery and thematic depth	Oliver invites readers to delve into themes of change and resilience by crafting a rich tapestry of imagery that parallels the sea's lessons with life's trials.
3.10	Visited Seaview's shores	The vivid imagery and emotional depth in Oliver's poetry are so immersive that readers feel as though they have experienced the coastal town firsthand.
3.11	Irony	Jenna explores themes of identity and belonging in her novel using irony, presenting situations or statements that imply a discrepancy between appearances and underlying truths.
3.12	Concise dialogue and vivid descriptions	Lumina's portrayal through concise dialogue and vivid descriptions creates a dynamic and detailed setting that reflects the city's dual nature.
3.13	Asking them to see beyond urban life's facade	'Shadows of Lumina' challenges readers by critiquing urban life's superficial aspects and urging them to consider deeper issues of identity and belonging.
3.14	A thematic depth	The paradoxes of Lumina reflected in the characters serve to deepen the narrative, illustrating complex themes through their experiences and contrasts.
3.15	Reflects personal struggles and triumphs	The novel acts as a mirror, reflecting readers' inner conflicts and victories, suggesting that it resonates on a personal level with themes of light and darkness.
3.16	Blending poetry with prose	Theo's lyrical style, which mixes poetry with prose, captures the festival's magical essence, using a fluid and expressive narrative form that enhances the storytelling.
3.17	Nostalgic and hopeful	Theo's narrative voice combines a longing for the past with an optimistic outlook, reflecting the festival's celebratory yet reflective nature.
3.18	The commercialization of traditional celebrations	Through satire, Theo critiques how traditional events have become commercialized, using humor to comment on the loss of their original significance.

3.19	A celebration of light amidst darkness	The novel mirrors the festival's dual nature as both a source of joy and a reminder of life's darker moments, symbolizing hope and resilience.
3.20	By describing the festival's lights and colors	Theo's vivid descriptions of the festival make its beauty and atmosphere leap off the page, allowing readers to visualize the event's enchanting display.
3.21	The dynamic nature of the city	Layla's use of stark contrasts in her graphic novel emphasizes the city's fluctuating atmosphere, showcasing its vibrant and shadowy sides.
3.22	Highlight the artwork's expressiveness	The minimalistic dialogue focuses attention on the artwork's ability to convey complex emotions and narratives, making each frame more impactful.
3.23	Isolation in a crowded city	The graphic novel captures the paradox of feeling alone despite being surrounded by people, highlighting urban life's inherent contradictions.
3.24	The mundane	Layla challenges readers to see the extraordinary in everyday urban settings, finding beauty and stories in the seemingly ordinary aspects of city life.
3.25	Using expressive artwork and minimalistic dialogue	The graphic novel conveys depth through its visual storytelling and sparing use of words, relying on the artwork to communicate themes and emotions.
3.26	Lyrical and imagery-rich	Nora's narrative style is marked by its musical quality and rich use of imagery, drawing readers into the sensory experiences of the countryside.
3.27	Emotional connections to the land	Nora explores the concept of home as an emotional bond with the land, emphasizing how personal identities are intertwined with their environments.
3.28	The bond between humans and nature	Nora's memoir pays homage to the enduring connection between people and the natural world, celebrating the deep ties that bind them.
3.29	Through the use of vivid imagery	Nora uses descriptive language to immerse readers in the countryside's beauty, allowing them to experience its tranquility and splendor as if they were there.
3.30	A feeling rooted in the heart	The memoir depicts home as an emotional state, deeply connected to the land and its stories, rather than a specific physical place.
3.31	Satire and dramatic irony	Aaron employs satire and dramatic irony to explore urban life, using humor and contradiction to critique societal norms and city living's absurdities.
3.32	Highlight the city's diversity	The dialogues and monologues in Aaron's play illuminate the varied experiences of the city's inhabitants, showcasing the multiplicity of urban life.
3.33	The unheard voices of the city	Aaron's play gives voice to the marginalized and overlooked aspects of urban existence, bringing attention to those often ignored in the broader societal narrative.
3.34	The complexities of society	'Voices of New Haven' uses the stage as a reflective surface to expose societal intricacies, encouraging the audience to contemplate the nature of community and individual roles within it.
3.35	Insight into human nature and society	Aaron's ability to highlight urban life's contradictions and challenges showcases his deep understanding of human nature and the societal fabric.
3.36	Enhance the mystery and complexity	Maya's narrative techniques add layers to the storytelling, making the plot more intricate and engaging the reader in actively piecing together the story.
3.37	Requires readers to engage actively	The use of metaphors and symbolism in Maya's writing demands active participation from readers to uncover the deeper meanings and connections within the narrative.
3.38	Knowledge, power, and truth	Maya's novel delves into profound themes, questioning the nature of knowledge, the dynamics of power, and the essence of truth through its storytelling.
3.39	Transcend time and invite exploration	'The Manuscript of Ages' underscores the enduring impact of stories, encouraging readers to explore beyond the surface and reflect on larger existential themes.
3.40	Through innovative narrative techniques	Maya's inventive storytelling approach, including nonlinear progression and diverse viewpoints, invites readers into the complex world of her narrative, enhancing the immersive experience.

Topic 4 - Evaluating Arguments and Persuasion

In the vibrant town of Greenfield, a debate was stirring among its residents. The town council proposed a new park, arguing it would provide a green space for community gatherings and promote outdoor activities. However, local business owners were concerned about the potential loss of parking spaces and increased traffic. At the town hall meeting, council members and business owners presented their arguments. The council emphasized the health and social benefits of the park, using statistics and examples from similar projects in other towns. Meanwhile, the business owners highlighted the potential economic impact, citing studies and surveys. The townspeople of Greenfield found themselves evaluating not just the arguments but the persuasive techniques used by both sides.

4.1) What evidence did the town council use to support their argument for the new park?

☐ Quotes from famous authors

☐ Statistics and examples from other towns

☐ Personal anecdotes

☐ Predictions of future events

4.2) The business owners' concern about parking and traffic is an example of:

☐ Exaggeration

☐ Logical reasoning

☐ Personal bias

☐ Appeal to emotion

4.3) Which persuasive technique did the council use to emphasize the benefits of the park?

☐ Presenting hypothetical scenarios

☐ Providing statistical evidence

☐ Using expert opinions

☐ Appealing to traditions

4.4) How did the business owners argue against the park's construction?

☐ Appealing to fear

☐ Using studies and surveys

☐ By criticizing the council members

☐ Offering alternative locations

4.5) Evaluating the arguments in the town hall meeting requires considering:

☐ The evidence and persuasive techniques used

☐ The personal opinions of the townspeople

☐ The popularity of the speakers

☐ The length of each argument

In Fairview High School, a heated discussion arose over the introduction of school uniforms. The principal argued that uniforms would create a more focused educational environment and reduce socio-economic disparities. In contrast, the student body, led by student president Mia, argued that uniforms would suppress individual expression and were unnecessary. During the school debate, the principal cited studies showing improved academic performance in schools with uniforms, while Mia presented surveys demonstrating student opposition to the idea. This debate challenged the students to critically assess not just the content of the arguments, but also the persuasive strategies employed by both sides.

4.6) What evidence did the principal use to support the introduction of uniforms?

☐ Personal opinions

☐ Historical data

☐ Studies on academic performance

☐ Student anecdotes

4.7) Mia's argument against uniforms focused on their impact on:

☐ Individual expression

☐ Teachers' workload

☐ School budget

☐ Academic subjects

4.8) The principal's reasoning for uniforms addressing socio-economic disparities is an example of:

☐ Appeal to authority

☐ Logical reasoning

☐ Appeal to tradition

☐ Emotional appeal

4.9) How did Mia demonstrate student opposition to uniforms?

☐ By staging a protest

☐ Writing an article

☐ Creating a petition

☐ Presenting surveys

4.10) Evaluating the school debate requires considering:

☐ The popularity of the speakers

☐ The length of the debate

☐ The evidence and persuasive techniques used

☐ The personal opinions of the audience

At Maplewood Community Center, a proposal to convert part of the public library into a digital learning center sparked debate among the residents. Proponents, led by librarian Mrs. Ellis, argued that the digital center would provide modern learning resources and bridge the digital divide. Opponents, however, feared that this would reduce the physical book collection and limit access for those less tech-savvy. In a community meeting, Mrs. Ellis presented data on increased usage in libraries with digital centers, while opponents shared testimonials from patrons who valued traditional resources. The debate highlighted the need for critical evaluation of both the data-driven approach and the emotional appeals presented.

4.11) What was Mrs. Ellis's main argument for converting part of the library?

☐ To attract younger patrons

☐ To create more space

☐ To reduce operating costs

☐ To provide modern learning resources

4.12) The opponents' concern about reducing the physical book collection is based on:

☐ Historical significance

☐ Emotional appeal

☐ Technological advancements

☐ Financial implications

4.13) Mrs. Ellis's use of data on library usage is an example of:

☐ Logical reasoning

☐ Appeal to authority

☐ Appeal to tradition

☐ Personal bias

4.14) How did the opponents argue their point in the meeting?

☐ By staging a demonstration

☐ Citing scientific studies

☐ Presenting a cost analysis

☐ Sharing testimonials from patrons

4.15) Evaluating the community center debate involves considering:

☐ The persuasiveness of the arguments

☐ The duration of the meeting

☐ The financial status of the speakers

☐ The number of people attending

In the coastal town of Harborview, the local government proposed a ban on plastic bags to reduce pollution. This initiative sparked a debate among the townspeople. Environmental activists, led by Dr. Greene, supported the ban, presenting research on the environmental impact of plastic waste. Local shop owners, however, argued that the ban would inconvenience customers and hurt small businesses. They suggested alternative solutions like promoting reusable bags. At a town forum, both sides presented their cases, with Dr. Greene using visual aids to show the damage caused by plastic, while shop owners shared stories of struggling businesses. The residents of Harborview had to weigh the arguments and assess the validity of the evidence and emotional appeals used.

4.16) What evidence did Dr. Greene present to support the plastic bag ban?

☐ Research on environmental impact

☐ Opinions of famous celebrities

☐ Financial statistics of the town

☐ Historical data on plastic usage

4.17) The shop owners' argument against the ban is primarily based on:

☐ Technological challenges

☐ Economic impact on businesses

☐ Legal implications

☐ Environmental concerns

4.18) Dr. Greene's use of visual aids to show plastic damage is an example of:

☐ Appeal to emotion

☐ Personal bias

☐ Exaggeration

☐ Logical reasoning

4.19) How did the shop owners propose to address the plastic problem?

☐ Increasing plastic bag prices

☐ Promoting reusable bags

☐ By ignoring it

☐ Outsourcing bag production

4.20) Evaluating the town forum's debate involves assessing:

☐ The length of each presentation

☐ The evidence and persuasive techniques used

☐ The age of the participants

☐ The size of the audience

In the small mountain town of Pine Ridge, a proposal to expand the ski resort into the neighboring forest raised concerns. The resort owners argued that the expansion would boost tourism and the local economy. Environmentalists, led by Ms. Taylor, opposed the expansion, citing the potential harm to wildlife habitats and the ecosystem. During a community forum, the resort owners presented economic growth projections and testimonials from other resort towns, while Ms. Taylor showcased studies on environmental impact and petitions from concerned citizens. The residents of Pine Ridge were tasked with analyzing the arguments, discerning biases, and evaluating the credibility of the sources presented by both sides.

4.21) What argument did the resort owners use to support the expansion?

☐ Improving public safety

☐ Promoting outdoor activities

☐ Economic growth and tourism

☐ Environmental conservation

4.22) Ms. Taylor's opposition to the expansion was based on:

☐ Traffic congestion concerns

☐ Potential harm to wildlife and the ecosystem

☐ The cost of construction

☐ The impact on resort aesthetics

4.23) The resort owners used which of the following to persuade the community?

☐ Historical data about ski resorts

☐ Economic growth projections and testimonials

☐ Personal stories of resort employees

☐ Scientific research on snowfall

4.24) How did Ms. Taylor demonstrate the environmental impact of the expansion?

☐ By organizing a protest

☐ Showing photos of the resort

☐ Interviewing tourists

☐ Presenting studies and petitions

4.25) Evaluating the community forum debate requires considering:

☐ The entertainment value of the debate

☐ The duration of each presentation

☐ The evidence and biases in the arguments

☐ The number of supporters for each side

In the bustling market district of Easton, a debate erupted over the city's plan to pedestrianize the main street. The city council claimed that pedestrianization would reduce pollution and increase foot traffic for businesses. However, some local shopkeepers were skeptical, arguing it would decrease accessibility for customers who drive and potentially hurt sales. At a public forum, the council presented data on improved business in similar pedestrian areas, while shopkeepers shared stories of struggling businesses in other cities that implemented similar changes. The residents of Easton were challenged to assess the strength of the arguments, considering the credibility of sources and the effectiveness of the persuasive strategies used.

4.26) What benefit did the city council cite for pedestrianizing the main street?

☐ Enhancing vehicle traffic flow

☐ Lowering real estate prices

☐ Creating more parking spaces

☐ Reducing pollution and increasing foot traffic

4.27) The shopkeepers' skepticism about pedestrianization was based on:

☐ Concerns about decreased accessibility and sales

☐ A preference for modern architecture

☐ The need for more green spaces

☐ The cost of street maintenance

4.28) In the public forum, how did the city council argue their point?

☐ Showing artistic renderings of the plan

☐ By presenting data on improved business

☐ Comparing with international cities

☐ Using celebrities' endorsements

4.29) How did the shopkeepers challenge the pedestrianization plan?

☐ Offering alternative city plans

☐ Citing historical traditions

☐ Sharing stories of struggling businesses

☐ Conducting a customer survey

4.30) Evaluating the Easton market debate involves:

☐ Counting the number of supporters for each side

☐ Judging the professionalism of the speakers

☐ Assessing the visual appeal of the presentations

☐ Considering the credibility of sources and persuasive strategies

In the suburban community of Oakdale, a new zoning proposal to allow the construction of a shopping center was the talk of the town. Advocates, including the developer Mr. Johnson, argued that the shopping center would create jobs and bring more business to Oakdale. However, a group of residents, led by Ms. Larson, raised concerns about increased traffic and the impact on small local businesses. At a town council meeting, Mr. Johnson presented economic projections, while Ms. Larson brought in small business owners to speak about potential negative effects. The Oakdale residents had to critically evaluate both sides, considering the evidence presented and the persuasive techniques used.

4.31) What was Mr. Johnson's main argument for building the shopping center?

☐ Improving public transport

☐ Creation of jobs and business growth

☐ Environmental benefits

☐ Cultural enrichment

4.32) Ms. Larson's group opposed the shopping center due to concerns about:

☐ Lack of entertainment options

☐ Health and safety regulations

☐ Architectural design

☐ Increased traffic and impact on local businesses

4.33) In the town council meeting, how did Mr. Johnson support his argument?

☐ Presenting economic projections

☐ Providing testimonials from celebrities

☐ Showing architectural plans

☐ Using historical data

4.34) How did Ms. Larson's group challenge the proposal?

☐ Organizing a protest

☐ Creating a social media campaign

☐ Bringing in small business owners to speak

☐ Conducting a public poll

4.35) Evaluating the Oakdale zoning debate involves:

☐ Analyzing the length of the speeches

☐ Considering the attire of the speakers

☐ Assessing the evidence and persuasive strategies used

☐ Counting the number of attendees

In Rivertown, a proposal to build a new dam sparked controversy among the residents. The town's mayor, Mr. Andrews, argued that the dam would provide renewable energy and reduce electricity costs. Environmental groups, led by Dr. Rivera, opposed the construction, claiming it would disrupt local ecosystems and displace wildlife. At a community hearing, Mr. Andrews presented technical data and cost-benefit analyses, while Dr. Rivera brought in environmental experts and wildlife biologists to discuss the ecological impact. The citizens of Rivertown faced the challenge of evaluating complex arguments, discerning fact from opinion, and understanding the persuasive tactics used by both sides.

4.36) What was Mr. Andrews' primary argument for building the dam?

☐ Improving water supply

☐ Creating new jobs

☐ Enhancing tourism

☐ Providing renewable energy and lowering costs

4.37) Dr. Rivera's opposition to the dam focused on:

☐ Potential for flooding

☐ Architectural design

☐ Disruption of local ecosystems

☐ Economic concerns

4.38) At the hearing, Mr. Andrews supported his argument with:

☐ Technical data and cost-benefit analyses

☐ Surveys of local residents

☐ Anecdotes from other towns

☐ Endorsements from politicians

4.39) Environmental experts at the hearing discussed the dam's impact on:

☐ Wildlife and ecosystems

☐ Recreational activities

☐ Traffic patterns

☐ Real estate prices

4.40) Evaluating the Rivertown dam debate involves:

☐ Counting the number of arguments presented

☐ Assessing the arguments' complexity and persuasiveness

☐ Considering the speakers' backgrounds

☐ Analyzing the visual aids used

Topic 4 - Answers

Question Number	Answer	Explanation
4.1	Statistics and examples from other towns	The town council used statistical evidence and examples from other towns to demonstrate the potential benefits of the new park.
4.2	Logical reasoning	The business owners used logical reasoning to express their concerns about parking and traffic issues that could arise.
4.3	Providing statistical evidence	The council used statistical evidence to support their claims about the health and social benefits of the park.
4.4	Using studies and surveys	The business owners argued against the park by using studies and surveys to highlight potential economic impacts.
4.5	The evidence and persuasive techniques used	Assessing the town hall meeting's arguments involves analyzing the evidence presented and the persuasive techniques employed.
4.6	Studies on academic performance	The principal used studies showing improved academic performance in schools with uniforms to support their argument.
4.7	Individual expression	Mia focused on the impact of uniforms on individual expression, arguing that they would suppress it.
4.8	Logical reasoning	The principal's argument about socio-economic disparities employs logical reasoning to support the introduction of uniforms.
4.9	Presenting surveys	Mia demonstrated student opposition to uniforms by presenting surveys that showed their views on the matter.
4.10	The evidence and persuasive techniques used	Evaluating the school debate requires considering the arguments' content and the persuasive strategies used by both sides.
4.11	To provide modern learning resources	Mrs. Ellis argued that the digital center would offer modern learning resources and bridge the digital divide.
4.12	Emotional appeal	The opponents' concerns about reducing physical books are based on emotional appeal, emphasizing the value of traditional resources.
4.13	Logical reasoning	Mrs. Ellis used logical reasoning by presenting data on increased library usage due to digital centers.
4.14	Sharing testimonials from patrons	The opponents argued their point by sharing testimonials from patrons who valued traditional library resources.
4.15	The persuasiveness of the arguments	Evaluating the debate involves assessing the persuasiveness of the arguments and the evidence presented.
4.16	Research on environmental impact	Dr. Greene supported the plastic bag ban by presenting research on the environmental impact of plastic waste.
4.17	Economic impact on businesses	Shop owners argued against the ban based on its potential economic impact on businesses.
4.18	Appeal to emotion	Dr. Greene's use of visual aids to show the damage caused by plastic is an appeal to emotion, highlighting environmental harm.

4.19	Promoting reusable bags	The shop owners proposed promoting reusable bags as an alternative solution to the plastic problem.
4.20	The evidence and persuasive techniques used	Evaluating the town forum's debate involves assessing the evidence presented and the effectiveness of the persuasive strategies used.
4.21	Economic growth and tourism	The resort owners supported the expansion by arguing it would boost tourism and the local economy.
4.22	Potential harm to wildlife and the ecosystem	Ms. Taylor opposed the expansion due to its potential environmental impact, particularly on wildlife and the ecosystem.
4.23	Economic growth projections and testimonials	The resort owners used economic growth projections and testimonials to persuade the community of the expansion's benefits.
4.24	Presenting studies and petitions	Ms. Taylor demonstrated the environmental impact by presenting relevant studies and petitions from concerned citizens.
4.25	The evidence and biases in the arguments	Evaluating the debate requires considering the arguments' evidence and any biases present in the viewpoints expressed.
4.26	Reducing pollution and increasing foot traffic	The city council cited reduced pollution and increased foot traffic for businesses as benefits of pedestrianizing the main street.
4.27	Concerns about decreased accessibility and sales	Shopkeepers were skeptical about pedestrianization due to potential decreases in accessibility for driving customers and potential impact on sales.
4.28	By presenting data on improved business	The city council argued their point by presenting data showing that similar pedestrian areas improved business.
4.29	Sharing stories of struggling businesses	Shopkeepers challenged the plan by sharing stories of businesses that struggled in other cities with similar pedestrianization.
4.30	Considering the credibility of sources and persuasive strategies	Evaluating the debate involves assessing the strength of the arguments, the credibility of sources, and the effectiveness of persuasive strategies used.
4.31	Creation of jobs and business growth	Mr. Johnson argued for the shopping center by citing its potential to create jobs and promote business growth in Oakdale.
4.32	Increased traffic and impact on local businesses	Ms. Larson and her group opposed the shopping center due to concerns about increased traffic and its impact on local businesses.
4.33	Presenting economic projections	Mr. Johnson supported his argument for the shopping center by presenting economic projections showing potential benefits.
4.34	Bringing in small business owners to speak	Ms. Larson challenged the proposal by bringing in small business owners to discuss the potential negative effects on their businesses.
4.35	Assessing the evidence and persuasive strategies used	Evaluating the Oakdale zoning debate involves considering the evidence presented and the persuasive techniques employed by both sides.
4.36	Providing renewable energy and lowering costs	Mr. Andrews argued for building the dam as a means to provide renewable energy and reduce electricity costs for Rivertown.
4.37	Disruption of local ecosystems	Dr. Rivera focused on the potential ecological disruption, such as harm to wildlife habitats, as a primary reason to oppose the dam.
4.38	Technical data and cost-benefit analyses	Mr. Andrews supported his pro-dam argument with technical data and analyses showing the projected benefits and costs of the dam.
4.39	Wildlife and ecosystems	Environmental experts discussed the impact of the dam on local wildlife and ecosystems, emphasizing potential ecological harm.
4.40	Assessing the arguments' complexity and persuasiveness	Evaluating the Rivertown dam debate involves analyzing the complexity of the arguments and their persuasiveness, as well as discerning fact from opinion.

Topic 5 - Word Definitions

5.1) What is the meaning of the word 'abhor'?

☐ to accept with enthusiasm

☐ capable of bending easily without breaking

☐ to dismantle or take apart

☐ to regard with disgust and hatred

5.2) What is the meaning of the word 'construct'?

☐ to accept with enthusiasm

☐ to build or form by putting together parts

☐ characterized by uncertainty or inaccuracy

☐ capable of bending easily without breaking

5.3) What is the meaning of the word 'precise'?

☐ to accept with enthusiasm

☐ characterized by uncertainty or inaccuracy

☐ capable of bending easily without breaking

☐ marked by exactness and accuracy of expression or detail

5.4) What is the meaning of the word 'abrasive'?

☐ showing little concern for the feelings of others; harsh

☐ to accept with enthusiasm

☐ capable of bending easily without breaking

☐ to merge or blend into a harmonious whole

5.5) What is the meaning of the word 'contrast'?

☐ capable of bending easily without breaking

☐ to accept with enthusiasm

☐ to compare in order to show differences

☐ to dismantle or take apart

5.6) What is the meaning of the word 'alternative'?

☐ clear and precise; leaving no room for confusion

☐ a sudden, unplanned course of action

☐ limited to certain individuals or groups

☐ offering or expressing a choice; different from the usual or conventional

5.7) What is the meaning of the word 'corroborate'?

☐ clear and precise; leaving no room for confusion

☐ limited to certain individuals or groups

☐ to confirm or give support to a statement, theory, or finding

☐ to contradict or disprove

5.8) What is the meaning of the word 'prevalent'?

☐ clear and precise; leaving no room for confusion

☐ limited to certain individuals or groups

☐ widespread in a particular area or at a particular time

☐ to contradict or disprove

5.9) What is the meaning of the word 'ambiguous'?

☐ open to more than one interpretation; not having one obvious meaning

☐ to contradict or disprove

☐ a sudden, unplanned course of action

☐ clear and precise; leaving no room for confusion

5.10) What is the meaning of the word 'procedure'?

☐ to contradict or disprove

☐ an established or official way of doing something

☐ limited to certain individuals or groups

☐ a sudden, unplanned course of action

5.11) What is the meaning of the word 'anarchy'?

☐ a state of disorder due to absence or nonrecognition of authority

☐ a person without any property

☐ to agree with or support

☐ an organized and peaceful society

5.12) What is the meaning of the word 'despicable'?

☐ to agree with or support

☐ worthy of praise and admiration

☐ an organized and peaceful society

☐ deserving hatred and contempt

5.13) What is the meaning of the word 'proprietor'?

☐ worthy of praise and admiration

☐ to agree with or support

☐ a person without any property

☐ the owner of a business, or a holder of property

5.14) What is the meaning of the word 'pseudonym'?

☐ a fictitious name, especially one used by an author

☐ a person without any property

☐ to agree with or support

☐ worthy of praise and admiration

5.15) What is the meaning of the word 'rebuke'?

☐ an organized and peaceful society

☐ to express sharp disapproval or criticism of someone because of their behavior or actions

☐ a well-known and established brand

☐ to agree with or support

5.16) What is the meaning of the word 'apprehend'?

☐ to end or terminate

☐ a person who strictly follows rules

☐ careless and impulsive

☐ to understand or perceive

5.17) What is the meaning of the word 'despondent'?

☐ to disregard or ignore

☐ to end or terminate

☐ in low spirits from loss of hope or courage

☐ filled with excitement and energy

5.18) What is the meaning of the word 'prudent'?

☐ a person who strictly follows rules

☐ to disregard or ignore

☐ acting with or showing care and thought for the future

☐ careless and impulsive

5.19) What is the meaning of the word 'embark'?

☐ a person who strictly follows rules

☐ filled with excitement and energy

☐ begin a course of action, especially one that is important

☐ careless and impulsive

5.20) What is the meaning of the word 'rebel'?

☐ filled with excitement and energy

☐ to disregard or ignore

☐ a person who resists authority, control, or tradition

☐ to end or terminate

5.21) What is the meaning of the word 'assimilate'?

☐ to agree with or support

☐ impossible to achieve or impractical

☐ to absorb and integrate into a wider society or culture

☐ a personal opinion or assumption

5.22) What is the meaning of the word 'evidence'?

☐ impossible to achieve or impractical

☐ a personal opinion or assumption

☐ the available body of facts or information indicating whether a belief or proposition is true or valid

☐ to reject or oppose

5.23) What is the meaning of the word 'rebuke'?

☐ to reject or oppose

☐ to agree with or support

☐ a personal opinion or assumption

☐ to express sharp disapproval or criticism of someone because of their behavior or actions

5.24) What is the meaning of the word 'audacious'?

☐ a personal opinion or assumption

☐ to reject or oppose

☐ showing a willingness to take surprisingly bold risks

☐ showing a reluctance to take risks

5.25) What is the meaning of the word 'feasible'?

□ a personal opinion or assumption

□ to reject or oppose

□ possible to do easily or conveniently

□ to agree with or support

5.26) What is the meaning of the word 'authority'?

□ the outer edge or margin

□ to officially endorse or support

□ an unsolicited opinion or reaction

□ the power or right to give orders, make decisions, and enforce obedience

5.27) What is the meaning of the word 'focus'?

□ the center of interest or activity

□ to officially endorse or support

□ the lack of power or influence

□ a group of objects produced at the same time

5.28) What is the meaning of the word 'response'?

□ an unsolicited opinion or reaction

□ a verbal or written answer

□ a group of objects produced at the same time

□ to officially endorse or support

5.29) What is the meaning of the word 'ban'?

☐ the lack of power or influence

☐ to officially or legally prohibit something

☐ an unsolicited opinion or reaction

☐ to officially endorse or support

5.30) What is the meaning of the word 'generation'?

☐ a group of objects produced at the same time

☐ all of the people born and living at about the same time, collectively

☐ the lack of power or influence

☐ the outer edge or margin

5.31) What is the meaning of the word 'reverberate'?

☐ pleasant and appealing

☐ friendly and peace-loving

☐ to remain constant and unchanging

☐ to be repeated several times as an echo

5.32) What is the meaning of the word 'belligerent'?

☐ completely different in nature

☐ friendly and peace-loving

☐ hostile and aggressive

☐ to remain constant and unchanging

5.33) What is the meaning of the word 'bisect'?

☐ to merge or combine

☐ to divide into two parts

☐ friendly and peace-loving

☐ to remain constant and unchanging

5.34) What is the meaning of the word 'gruesome'?

☐ completely different in nature

☐ friendly and peace-loving

☐ causing repulsion or horror; grisly

☐ pleasant and appealing

5.35) What is the meaning of the word 'similar'?

☐ to remain constant and unchanging

☐ completely different in nature

☐ resembling without being identical

☐ to merge or combine

5.36) What is the meaning of the word 'prevalent'?

☐ to disappear completely or permanently

☐ widespread in a particular area at a particular time

☐ to accept or welcome with enthusiasm

☐ to create or originate

5.37) What is the meaning of the word 'elapse'?

☐ to pass or go by (used of time)

☐ to disappear completely or permanently

☐ to create or originate

☐ rarely encountered or seen

5.38) What is the meaning of the word 'quote'?

☐ to repeat or copy out (a group of words from a text or speech)

☐ to remain static or unchanged

☐ rarely encountered or seen

☐ to disappear completely or permanently

5.39) What is the meaning of the word 'rebuff'?

☐ rarely encountered or seen

☐ to disappear completely or permanently

☐ to reject (someone or something) in an abrupt or ungracious manner

☐ to accept or welcome with enthusiasm

5.40) What is the meaning of the word 'recur'?

☐ to occur again, periodically or repeatedly

☐ to remain static or unchanged

☐ to disappear completely or permanently

☐ to accept or welcome with enthusiasm

Topic 5 - Answers

Question Number	Answer	Explanation
5.1	To regard with disgust and hatred	'Abhor' means to have a strong feeling of disgust and hatred.
5.2	To build or form by putting together parts	'Construct' means to build something by putting parts together.
5.3	Marked by exactness and accuracy of expression or detail	'Precise' means being exact and accurate in expression or detail.
5.4	Showing little concern for the feelings of others; harsh	'Abrasive' refers to a personality that is harsh and shows little concern for others' feelings.
5.5	To compare in order to show differences	'Contrast' means to compare things to highlight their differences.
5.6	Offering or expressing a choice; different from the usual or conventional	'Alternative' refers to something that offers a choice or is different from the norm.
5.7	To confirm or give support to a statement, theory, or finding	'Corroborate' means to provide evidence or information that supports a statement, theory, or finding.
5.8	Widespread in a particular area or at a particular time	'Prevalent' means being widespread in a certain area or time.
5.9	Open to more than one interpretation; not having one obvious meaning	'Ambiguous' means having more than one possible interpretation or meaning.
5.10	An established or official way of doing something	'Procedure' refers to an established way of doing something, especially in a systematic way.
5.11	A state of disorder due to absence or nonrecognition of authority	'Anarchy' means a state of disorder due to the absence or non-recognition of authority.
5.12	Deserving hatred and contempt	'Despicable' means deserving of hatred and contempt.
5.13	The owner of a business, or a holder of property	'Proprietor' means someone who owns a business or holds property.
5.14	A fictitious name, especially one used by an author	'Pseudonym' is a fictitious name used by an author or other individual, especially for privacy or anonymity.
5.15	To express sharp disapproval or criticism of someone because of their behavior or actions	'Rebuke' means to express sharp disapproval or criticism of someone's behavior or actions.
5.16	To understand or perceive	'Apprehend' means to understand or grasp the meaning of something.
5.17	In low spirits from loss of hope or courage	'Despondent' describes someone who is in low spirits due to loss of hope or courage.
5.18	Acting with or showing care and thought for the future	'Prudent' means showing care and thought for the future.

5.19	Begin a course of action, especially one that is important	'Embark' means to start a significant course of action or journey.
5.20	A person who resists authority, control, or tradition	'Rebel' refers to someone who resists or defies authority, control, or tradition.
5.21	To absorb and integrate into a wider society or culture	'Assimilate' means to absorb and incorporate into a broader society or culture.
5.22	The available body of facts or information indicating whether a belief or proposition is true or valid	'Evidence' is the collection of facts or information indicating whether a belief or proposition is true or valid.
5.23	To express sharp disapproval or criticism of someone because of their behavior or actions	'Rebuke' means to express sharp disapproval or criticism of someone's actions or behavior.
5.24	Showing a willingness to take surprisingly bold risks	'Audacious' describes being willing to take surprisingly bold risks.
5.25	Possible to do easily or conveniently	'Feasible' means something that is possible and easy or convenient to do.
5.26	The power or right to give orders, make decisions, and enforce obedience	'Authority' refers to the power to give orders, make decisions, and enforce obedience.
5.27	The center of interest or activity	'Focus' refers to the main point of interest or activity.
5.28	A verbal or written answer	'Response' is a verbal or written reply or answer.
5.29	To officially or legally prohibit something	'Ban' means to officially or legally prohibit something.
5.30	All of the people born and living at about the same time, collectively	'Generation' refers to all the people born and living around the same time, seen as a group.
5.31	To be repeated several times as an echo	'Reverberate' means to be repeated as an echo, usually several times.
5.32	Hostile and aggressive	'Belligerent' means showing hostility and aggression.
5.33	To divide into two parts	'Bisect' means to divide something into two parts.
5.34	Causing repulsion or horror; grisly	'Gruesome' describes something that causes horror or repulsion; it is grisly.
5.35	Resembling without being identical	'Similar' means resembling something without being exactly the same.
5.36	Widespread in a particular area at a particular time	'Prevalent' means being widespread in a certain area or at a certain time.
5.37	To pass or go by (used of time)	'Elapse' means for time to pass or go by.
5.38	To repeat or copy out (a group of words from a text or speech)	'Quote' means to repeat or copy out words from a text or speech.
5.39	To reject (someone or something) in an abrupt or ungracious manner	'Rebuff' means to abruptly or ungraciously reject someone or something.
5.40	To occur again, periodically or repeatedly	'Recur' means to happen again, either periodically or repeatedly.

Topic 6 – Reading Comprehension

In the small coastal town of Seaview, a young girl named Lily discovered an old, tattered map in her attic. The map, which belonged to her grandfather, a retired sea captain, was rumored to lead to a hidden treasure. Filled with curiosity and adventure, Lily decided to follow the map. Along her journey, she encountered various challenges like deciphering riddles and navigating through the dense forest. With each step, she learned more about her grandfather's past and the rich history of Seaview. Her determination and bravery helped her overcome these obstacles, leading her to discover not only the treasure but also the true value of perseverance and family heritage.

6.1) What motivated Lily to follow the old map?

☐ Her curiosity and sense of adventure

☐ Her friends' encouragement

☐ A dream she had

☐ A school assignment

6.2) What did Lily encounter on her journey?

☐ Riddles and dense forest

☐ Friendly animals

☐ A hidden village

☐ Her school friends

6.3) What did Lily learn about during her journey?

☐ Her grandfather's past and Seaview's history

☐ How to read a compass

☐ Different types of trees

☐ Marine biology

6.4) How did Lily overcome the challenges she faced?

□ Using a GPS device

□ With determination and bravery

□ With help from a mysterious stranger

□ By avoiding them

6.5) What did Lily ultimately discover at the end of her journey?

□ A lost family heirloom

□ The treasure and the value of perseverance

□ A new species of bird

□ An old shipwreck

Max, a young aspiring astronomer, spent his nights gazing at the stars from his backyard. One evening, he noticed a peculiar blinking light in the sky. Intrigued, he set out to investigate with his telescope and astronomy books. His exploration led him to learn about various celestial phenomena and constellations. As he delved deeper, Max discovered the light was from a rarely observed comet passing near Earth. Excited, he shared his findings with his school's science club, inspiring his peers to take interest in astronomy. Max's discovery not only deepened his love for the stars but also brought his community together to appreciate the wonders of the night sky.

6.6) What first caught Max's attention in the night sky?

□ A shooting star

□ A peculiar blinking light

□ A full moon

□ A passing airplane

6.7) What tools did Max use to investigate the light?

☐ A map and compass

☐ His telescope and astronomy books

☐ Binoculars and a notepad

☐ A camera and computer

6.8) What did Max learn about through his investigation?

☐ Weather patterns

☐ Airplane routes

☐ Celestial phenomena and constellations

☐ Bird migration

6.9) What was the source of the blinking light Max observed?

☐ A space station

☐ A satellite

☐ A rarely observed comet

☐ A distant planet

6.10) How did Max's discovery affect his school community?

☐ Led to a camping trip

☐ Inspired interest in astronomy

☐ Created a photography club

☐ Started a science fair

In the historical city of Oldbridge, a group of students embarked on a project to uncover its hidden past. Led by their history teacher, Mr. Thompson, they began exploring local archives and interviewing long-time residents. Their research uncovered stories about Oldbridge's founding, its role in significant historical events, and tales of legendary local figures. As the project progressed, the students created an exhibition displaying their findings, which attracted attention from the community and local media. The project not only brought history to life for the students but also instilled a sense of pride and connection to their city's heritage.

6.11) What was the objective of the students' project in Oldbridge?

☐ To uncover the city's hidden past

☐ To write a fiction story

☐ To plan a city festival

☐ To compete in a science fair

6.12) Who led the students in their historical research?

☐ A famous author

☐ Their history teacher, Mr. Thompson

☐ A local historian

☐ The city mayor

6.13) What did the students discover about Oldbridge?

☐ Its founding and historical significance

☐ Modern architectural designs

☐ Geographical landscapes

☐ Future development plans

6.14) How did the students share their findings with the community?

☐ By creating an exhibition

☐ Making a documentary film

☐ Publishing a book

☐ Through a theatrical play

6.15) What impact did the project have on the students and community?

☐ Increased interest in sports

☐ A desire to travel

☐ A sense of pride in their heritage

☐ A focus on technology

In the bustling city of Metroville, a group of friends discovered an old, abandoned theater. Fascinated by its history, they decided to explore it. Inside, they found old movie posters, antique projectors, and a collection of classic films. Intrigued by their discovery, they researched the theater's past and learned about its significance in the golden era of cinema. Inspired, they organized a film festival showcasing these classic films, inviting the community to relive the theater's glory days. This event not only revived interest in classic cinema but also sparked a movement to restore and preserve the historic theater.

6.16) What did the friends discover in the old theater?

☐ Modern art pieces

☐ Historical documents

☐ Old movie posters and classic films

☐ Ancient artifacts

6.17) What did the friends learn about the theater?

☐ Its significance in local politics

☐ Its role in the golden era of cinema

☐ Its architectural design

☐ Its use as a community center

6.18) What event did the friends organize?

☐ A photography exhibition

☐ A film festival showcasing classic films

☐ A historical tour of the city

☐ A theater renovation project

6.19) What was the impact of the film festival on the community?

☐ Revived interest in classic cinema

☐ Decline in theater attendance

☐ Rise in local tourism

☐ Increased focus on modern movies

6.20) What movement was sparked by the event?

☐ Restoration of the historic theater

☐ Building a new theater

☐ Creating a cinema school

☐ Starting a film production company

In the quiet village of Willow Creek, an ancient oak tree stood as a symbol of wisdom and endurance. The villagers believed the tree held magical properties and gathered annually to celebrate its existence. This year, a young girl named Emma, intrigued by the legends, decided to learn more about the tree. Her research led her to uncover tales of historical events, folklore, and ancestral wisdom connected to the oak. Motivated by her findings, Emma organized a community project to preserve the tree and its surrounding area, igniting a renewed sense of unity and respect for nature among the villagers.

6.21) What was the ancient oak tree in Willow Creek a symbol of?

☐ Strength and power

☐ Beauty and grace

☐ Wisdom and endurance

☐ Wealth and prosperity

6.22) What did Emma discover about the oak tree?

☐ Scientific facts

☐ Artistic inspiration

☐ Historical events and folklore

☐ Geographical significance

6.23) What project did Emma organize?

☐ Preservation of the tree and its area

☐ A music festival

☐ An art contest

☐ A tree planting campaign

6.24) How did the villagers view the oak tree?

☐ As a nuisance

☐ As a source of wood

☐ As a playground

☐ As having magical properties

6.25) What was the impact of Emma's project on the community?

☐ Renewed unity and respect for nature

☐ Economic growth

☐ Environmental concerns

☐ Increased tourism

In the bustling city of Greenfield, a group of students from Lincoln Middle School started a community garden project. Their aim was to transform a vacant lot into a vibrant space for growing vegetables and flowers. With guidance from their science teacher, Mrs. Clark, and support from local businesses, the students learned about botany, sustainability, and teamwork. As the garden flourished, it became a source of pride for the school and a beloved spot for community members. The project not only beautified the neighborhood but also taught valuable lessons about ecology, cooperation, and the impact of small actions on the environment.

6.26) What was the purpose of the community garden project?

☐ To beautify a vacant lot and learn about botany

☐ To set up an outdoor theater

☐ To build a new school building

☐ To create a sports field

6.27) Who helped the students in their gardening project?

☐ A famous chef

☐ An architect

☐ A professional gardener

☐ Their science teacher, Mrs. Clark

6.28) What did the garden become a source of for the school?

☐ A place for science experiments

☐ A new curriculum focus

☐ Pride and a community spot

☐ Income through produce sales

6.29) What lessons did the students learn from the project?

☐ Art and design

☐ Mathematics and engineering

☐ Ecology, cooperation, and environmental impact

☐ History and geography

6.30) How did local businesses contribute to the project?

☐ Providing support and resources

☐ Designing the garden layout

☐ Buying the produce

☐ Offering cooking classes

In the mountainous region of Highland Hills, a mysterious old mansion stood atop the highest peak. Local legend spoke of a hidden treasure within its walls. Curious about the legend, a group of friends, Alex, Jamie, and Sam, decided to explore the mansion. As they navigated through dusty rooms and secret passages, they encountered puzzles and clues left by the mansion's previous owner, an eccentric collector. The adventure led them to discover not only the treasure - a collection of rare artifacts - but also stories of the collector's travels and the history of Highland Hills. Their journey taught them the value of teamwork, courage, and the thrill of solving mysteries.

6.31) What was the local legend about the old mansion?

□ A haunted spirit

□ A hidden treasure within its walls

□ An ancient curse

□ A secret royal lineage

6.32) Who decided to explore the mansion?

□ A group of tourists

□ A team of archaeologists

□ Friends Alex, Jamie, and Sam

□ Local historians

6.33) What did the friends find in the mansion?

□ Modern technology

□ Historical documents

□ Puzzles and clues

□ Lost family heirlooms

6.34) What did the treasure turn out to be?

□ A collection of rare artifacts

□ Gold and jewels

□ Paintings and sculptures

□ Ancient manuscripts

6.35) What did the friends learn from their adventure?

□ Architectural design

□ Teamwork, courage, and the thrill of mystery

□ Cooking recipes

□ Gardening skills

In the futuristic city of Solaris, renowned for its advancements in renewable energy, a young inventor named Mia created a solar-powered robot named Sunny. Mia entered Sunny in the annual Solaris Tech Fair, hoping to demonstrate the potential of solar energy. During the fair, Sunny amazed the audience with its ability to harness sunlight for various tasks. However, a sudden storm threatened to ruin the presentation. Mia quickly adapted and showed how Sunny could also operate efficiently under limited light. This display of innovation won Mia the top prize and highlighted the importance of adaptability and sustainability in technology.

6.36) What was Mia's invention in the city of Solaris?

□ A new type of solar panel

□ A wind turbine

□ An electric car

□ A solar-powered robot named Sunny

6.37) What event did Mia participate in with her invention?

☐ A robotics competition

☐ A science conference

☐ An environmental rally

☐ The Solaris Tech Fair

6.38) How did Sunny impress the audience?

☐ By harnessing sunlight for tasks

☐ By painting pictures

☐ By solving complex math problems

☐ By performing musical numbers

6.39) What challenge did Mia face during the presentation?

☐ A sudden storm

☐ A power outage

☐ A rival competitor

☐ Technical malfunctions

6.40) What did Mia's success at the fair highlight?

☐ The superiority of solar energy

☐ The importance of adaptability in technology

☐ The need for more inventions

☐ The benefits of teamwork

Topic 6 - Answers

Question Number	Answer	Explanation
6.1	Her curiosity and sense of adventure	Lily was motivated by her curiosity and sense of adventure to follow the old map.
6.2	Riddles and dense forest	Lily encountered various challenges like deciphering riddles and navigating through dense forests.
6.3	Her grandfather's past and Seaview's history	During her journey, Lily learned more about her grandfather's past and the rich history of Seaview.
6.4	With determination and bravery	Lily overcame the challenges she faced with determination and bravery.
6.5	The treasure and the value of perseverance	Lily discovered not only the treasure but also the true value of perseverance and family heritage.
6.6	A peculiar blinking light	Max first noticed a peculiar blinking light in the sky.
6.7	His telescope and astronomy books	Max used his telescope and astronomy books to investigate the blinking light.
6.8	Celestial phenomena and constellations	Max learned about various celestial phenomena and constellations through his investigation.
6.9	A rarely observed comet	The source of the blinking light Max observed was a rarely observed comet.
6.10	Inspired interest in astronomy	Max's discovery inspired his peers to take interest in astronomy, affecting his school community.
6.11	To uncover the city's hidden past	The objective of the students' project in Oldbridge was to uncover the city's hidden past.
6.12	Their history teacher, Mr. Thompson	The students in Oldbridge were led in their historical research by their history teacher, Mr. Thompson.
6.13	Its founding and historical significance	The students discovered stories about Oldbridge's founding and its role in significant historical events.
6.14	By creating an exhibition	The students shared their findings with the community by creating an exhibition.
6.15	A sense of pride in their heritage	The project brought history to life for the students and instilled a sense of pride in their city's heritage.
6.16	Old movie posters and classic films	The friends discovered old movie posters and a collection of classic films in the old theater.
6.17	Its role in the golden era of cinema	The friends learned about the theater's significance in the golden era of cinema.
6.18	A film festival showcasing classic films	The friends organized a film festival showcasing these classic films.
6.19	Revived interest in classic cinema	The film festival revived interest in classic cinema among the community.

6.20	Restoration of the historic theater	The event sparked a movement to restore and preserve the historic theater.
6.21	Wisdom and endurance	The ancient oak tree in Willow Creek was a symbol of wisdom and endurance.
6.22	Historical events and folklore	Emma discovered tales of historical events and folklore connected to the oak tree.
6.23	Preservation of the tree and its area	Emma organized a community project to preserve the tree and its surrounding area.
6.24	As having magical properties	The villagers viewed the oak tree as having magical properties.
6.25	Renewed unity and respect for nature	Emma's project ignited a renewed sense of unity and respect for nature among the villagers.
6.26	To beautify a vacant lot and learn about botany	The purpose of the community garden project was to transform a vacant lot into a vibrant space for growing.
6.27	Their science teacher, Mrs. Clark	The students were helped in their gardening project by their science teacher, Mrs. Clark.
6.28	Pride and a community spot	The garden became a source of pride for the school and a beloved community spot.
6.29	Ecology, cooperation, and environmental impact	The students learned valuable lessons about ecology, cooperation, and environmental impact.
6.30	Providing support and resources	Local businesses contributed to the project by providing support and resources.
6.31	A hidden treasure within its walls	The local legend about the old mansion was that it contained a hidden treasure.
6.32	Friends Alex, Jamie, and Sam	Friends Alex, Jamie, and Sam decided to explore the mansion.
6.33	Puzzles and clues	The friends found puzzles and clues in the mansion left by the previous owner.
6.34	A collection of rare artifacts	The treasure turned out to be a collection of rare artifacts.
6.35	Teamwork, courage, and the thrill of mystery	The friends learned the value of teamwork, courage, and the thrill of solving mysteries.
6.36	A solar-powered robot named Sunny	Mia's invention in the city of Solaris was a solar-powered robot named Sunny.
6.37	The Solaris Tech Fair	Mia participated in the Solaris Tech Fair with her invention.
6.38	By harnessing sunlight for tasks	Sunny impressed the audience by harnessing sunlight for various tasks.
6.39	A sudden storm	Mia faced the challenge of a sudden storm during her presentation.
6.40	The importance of adaptability in technology	Mia's success at the fair highlighted the importance of adaptability and sustainability in technology.

Topic 7 – Character Analysis

In the vibrant city of Artville, a young artist named Emma struggled to find her artistic voice. Despite her talent, she often compared her work to others and felt discouraged. Her art teacher, Mr. Jenkins, noticed her struggle and encouraged her to explore various art styles. Inspired by his advice, Emma began experimenting and soon developed a unique style that blended traditional and modern techniques. Through her journey, Emma learned the importance of self-acceptance and individuality. Her final art project, a vivid representation of her growth, earned accolades at the school art show, marking a turning point in her confidence and artistic expression.

7.1) What was Emma's initial struggle as an artist?

☐ Time management

☐ Finding art supplies

☐ Finding her unique artistic style

☐ Lack of talent

7.2) How did Mr. Jenkins help Emma?

☐ By giving her extra classes

☐ By buying her art supplies

☐ By encouraging her to explore different art styles

☐ By introducing her to famous artists

7.3) What was the result of Emma's experimentation with art?

☐ Focusing on landscape paintings

☐ Deciding to quit art

☐ Switching to photography

☐ Development of a unique style

7.4) What did Emma learn through her artistic journey?

□ The business side of art

□ The need for better art tools

□ The importance of self-acceptance and individuality

□ The history of art

7.5) How was Emma's growth as an artist recognized?

□ Selling her art in a gallery

□ Winning an online contest

□ Earning accolades at the school art show

□ Being featured in a magazine

In the quiet town of Pine Ridge, young Leo discovered an old guitar in his grandmother's attic. Despite never having played before, Leo felt a deep connection with the instrument. He began teaching himself to play, facing challenges like sore fingers and complex chords. As he practiced, Leo's dedication impressed his family, and they supported him by attending his small performances. Leo's perseverance paid off when he was selected to perform at the town's music festival. Through his journey, Leo learned the value of persistence, the joy of music, and the importance of family support.

7.6) What did Leo discover in his grandmother's attic?

□ An old guitar

□ A vintage piano

□ A collection of records

□ A set of drums

7.7) What challenges did Leo face while learning the guitar?

☐ Buying guitar strings

☐ Finding a music teacher

☐ Sore fingers and complex chords

☐ Writing his own songs

7.8) How did Leo's family show support for his music?

☐ Attending his performances

☐ Buying him a new guitar

☐ Recording his music

☐ Signing him up for lessons

7.9) What opportunity did Leo earn through his dedication?

☐ Winning a music competition

☐ Joining a band

☐ Releasing an album

☐ Performing at the town's music festival

7.10) What did Leo learn from his experience with the guitar?

☐ How to write hit songs

☐ The value of persistence and importance of family support

☐ The history of music

☐ Technical aspects of sound production

In the bustling city of Riverport, a teenage detective named Sarah was known for her sharp mind and keen observation skills. When a mysterious case of disappearing artifacts from the local museum arose, Sarah took it upon herself to solve the mystery. She interviewed witnesses, gathered clues, and analyzed evidence with precision. Throughout her investigation, Sarah faced skepticism from the local police but remained determined. Her efforts led to the unveiling of an unexpected culprit, a respected museum curator. Sarah's journey showcased her resilience, intellect, and the ability to challenge perceptions, gaining respect and admiration from the community.

7.11) What was Sarah known for in Riverport?

☐ Her musical talent

☐ Her artistic creations

☐ Her detective skills and keen observation

☐ Her athletic abilities

7.12) What mystery did Sarah decide to solve?

☐ A missing person case

☐ A bank robbery

☐ The disappearance of artifacts from the museum

☐ A mysterious message

7.13) How did Sarah conduct her investigation?

☐ Relying on psychic predictions

☐ Interviewing witnesses and analyzing evidence

☐ Setting up surveillance cameras

☐ Using advanced technology

7.14) Who was revealed to be the culprit?

☐ A police officer

☐ A local artist

☐ Sarah's friend

☐ The museum curator

7.15) What did Sarah's journey showcase about her character?

☐ Shyness, indecision, and dependence

☐ Resilience, intellect, and challenging perceptions

☐ Fearlessness, impulsiveness, and recklessness

☐ Creativity, spontaneity, and unpredictability

In the peaceful village of Meadowfield, there lived a young boy named Lucas with a passion for astronomy. Despite his interest, Lucas was afraid of the dark, which made stargazing a challenge. With encouragement from his parents and his best friend Zoe, Lucas decided to face his fear. Each night, they would join him in the backyard, gradually helping him feel comfortable under the starlit sky. Lucas's journey was filled with moments of anxiety, joy, and wonder as he learned to overcome his fear. His first successful night of stargazing marked a significant personal achievement and deepened his love for the stars.

7.16) What was Lucas's passion and what challenge did he face?

☐ Astronomy and fear of the dark

☐ Sports and fear of failure

☐ Music and stage fright

☐ Art and lack of inspiration

7.17) Who helped Lucas overcome his fear?

☐ His siblings

☐ A professional astronomer

☐ His parents and friend Zoe

☐ His teacher

7.18) What did Lucas experience during his journey?

☐ Excitement, eagerness, and impatience

☐ Disappointment, anger, and frustration

☐ Confusion, boredom, and indifference

☐ Anxiety, joy, and wonder

7.19) What marked Lucas's first successful stargazing experience?

☐ Overcoming his fear of the dark

☐ Photographing the moon

☐ Spotting a shooting star

☐ Identifying a new constellation

7.20) How did facing his fear affect Lucas?

☐ It led him to change his interests

☐ It had no significant impact

☐ It deepened his love for astronomy

☐ It made him dislike stargazing

In the town of Harmony, there was a renowned music school known for its exceptional orchestra. Among its members was a talented violinist, Anna, who was highly competitive and often dismissive of her peers. Her attitude changed when a new conductor, Mr. Ellis, joined the school. He emphasized teamwork and the beauty of collaborative music, challenging Anna's perspective. Through various exercises and group performances, Anna began to appreciate her fellow musicians' talents and contributions. Her transformation from a solitary player to a team member not only improved the orchestra's performance but also enriched Anna's personal and musical growth.

7.21) What was Anna's initial attitude in the orchestra?

☐ Competitive and dismissive

☐ Supportive and collaborative

☐ Shy and reserved

☐ Indifferent and detached

7.22) How did the new conductor, Mr. Ellis, influence Anna?

☐ By emphasizing teamwork in music

☐ By giving her solo performances

☐ By ignoring her behavior

☐ By criticizing her skills

7.23) What change occurred in Anna after working with Mr. Ellis?

☐ She decided to quit the orchestra

☐ She focused only on solo pieces

☐ She became more competitive

☐ She valued her peers' talents more

7.24) What impact did Anna's transformation have on the orchestra?

☐ Increased conflicts among members

☐ No significant change

☐ Improved performance and unity

☐ Decreased quality of music

7.25) What did Anna gain from her experience in the orchestra?

☐ Personal and musical growth

☐ Fame and recognition

☐ A sense of superiority

☐ Financial success

In the coastal town of Clearwater, a young surfer named Jake dreamed of winning the national surfing championship. Known for his daring and aggressive style, Jake often took risks to outperform his competitors. However, his approach changed after meeting an experienced surfer, Mia, who taught him the value of patience and strategy in surfing. Under her mentorship, Jake learned to read the waves and adapt his techniques. This new approach not only improved his performance but also helped him win the championship. Jake's journey highlighted the evolution of his character from a reckless competitor to a strategic and thoughtful surfer.

7.26) What was Jake known for in surfing?

☐ His artistic moves

☐ His daring and aggressive style

☐ His slow and steady pace

☐ His cautious approach

7.27) How did meeting Mia influence Jake?

☐ Encouraged more risks

☐ Dissuaded him from competing

☐ Focused on physical fitness

☐ Taught him patience and strategy

7.28) What change occurred in Jake's surfing technique?

☐ Focusing solely on speed

☐ Adapting to the waves and refining techniques

☐ Avoiding challenging waves

☐ Relying on strength over skill

7.29) What was the outcome of Jake's new approach?

☐ Losing interest in surfing

☐ Starting a surfing school

☐ Deciding to retire from surfing

☐ Winning the national championship

7.30) What aspect of Jake's character evolved through his journey?

☐ From enthusiastic to apathetic

☐ From confident to uncertain

☐ From friendly to solitary

☐ From reckless to strategic and thoughtful

In the small village of Brookhaven, there was a shy and introverted girl named Lily who had a hidden talent for writing. Her classmates were unaware of her skill, as Lily was hesitant to share her stories. However, her teacher, Mrs. Evans, recognized Lily's potential and gently encouraged her to participate in the school's writing competition. Gradually, Lily gained confidence and submitted a story that captivated everyone. Her success not only won her the competition but also earned her newfound respect and friendship from her peers. This experience transformed Lily from a reserved individual to a confident and celebrated young writer in her community.

7.31) What was Lily's hidden talent?

☐ Singing

☐ Writing

☐ Painting

☐ Dancing

7.32) Who encouraged Lily to enter the writing competition?

☐ Her best friend

☐ Her parents

☐ A famous author

☐ Her teacher, Mrs. Evans

7.33) How did Lily's participation in the competition affect her?

☐ Gained confidence and won respect

☐ Decided to stop writing

☐ Became more introverted

☐ Faced criticism

7.34) What was the outcome of Lily's story submission?

☐ Being published in a magazine

☐ Winning the competition and earning friendships

☐ Inspiring a school play

☐ Receiving constructive feedback

7.35) How did Lily transform through her experience?

☐ From confident to doubtful

☐ From enthusiastic to disinterested

☐ From social to isolated

☐ From shy to confident and celebrated

In the bustling metropolis of Tech City, a young tech enthusiast named Alex dreamt of developing innovative software. Alex was known for his intelligence but was often impatient and dismissive of others' ideas. This attitude changed when he collaborated on a project with a diverse team of developers. During the project, Alex faced conflicts due to his approach, but gradually, he learned to value different perspectives and teamwork. This experience not only enhanced the software but also transformed Alex into a more empathetic and effective leader. His growth was evident when the team's project won an award for innovation, highlighting the power of collaboration.

7.36) What was Alex known for in Tech City?

☐ His intelligence and impatience

☐ His leadership and generosity

☐ His creativity and solitude

☐ His humor and laziness

7.37) What changed Alex's attitude towards teamwork?

☐ Receiving criticism from his boss

☐ Attending a leadership seminar

☐ Reading inspirational books

☐ Collaborating with a diverse team

7.38) How did Alex's approach to the project initially cause conflict?

☐ His overly relaxed attitude

☐ His lack of technical skills

☐ His dismissiveness of others' ideas

☐ His strict deadlines

7.39) What did Alex learn from working on the project?

☐ The value of different perspectives and teamwork

☐ The need for stricter project management

☐ The benefits of working alone

☐ The importance of being the sole decision-maker

7.40) What recognition did the team's project achieve?

☐ Media attention

☐ An award for innovation

☐ A patent for new technology

☐ Financial success

Topic 7 – Answers

Question Number	Answer	Explanation
7.1	Finding her unique artistic style	Emma initially struggled to find her unique artistic voice, feeling discouraged.
7.2	By encouraging her to explore different art styles	Mr. Jenkins helped Emma by encouraging her to experiment with various art styles.
7.3	Development of a unique style	Emma's experimentation led to the development of her unique style blending traditional and modern techniques.
7.4	The importance of self-acceptance and individuality	Through her journey, Emma learned the importance of self-acceptance and individuality.
7.5	Earning accolades at the school art show	Emma's growth was recognized by earning accolades at the school art show.
7.6	An old guitar	Leo discovered an old guitar in his grandmother's attic.
7.7	Sore fingers and complex chords	Leo faced challenges like sore fingers and learning complex chords while learning the guitar.
7.8	Attending his performances	Leo's family showed support by attending his small performances.
7.9	Performing at the town's music festival	Leo's perseverance paid off when he was selected to perform at the town's music festival.
7.10	The value of persistence and importance of family support	Leo learned the value of persistence and the importance of family support.
7.11	Her detective skills and keen observation	Sarah in Riverport was known for her sharp mind and keen observation skills.
7.12	The disappearance of artifacts from the museum	Sarah decided to solve the mystery of disappearing artifacts from the local museum.
7.13	Interviewing witnesses and analyzing evidence	Sarah conducted her investigation by interviewing witnesses and analyzing evidence.
7.14	The museum curator	The unexpected culprit revealed was the respected museum curator.
7.15	Resilience, intellect, and challenging perceptions	Sarah's journey showcased her resilience, intellect, and the ability to challenge perceptions.
7.16	Astronomy and fear of the dark	Lucas had a passion for astronomy but faced a challenge with his fear of the dark.
7.17	His parents and friend Zoe	Lucas was helped to overcome his fear by his parents and his best friend Zoe.
7.18	Anxiety, joy, and wonder	Lucas experienced moments of anxiety, joy, and wonder as he learned to overcome his fear.

7.19	Overcoming his fear of the dark	Lucas's first successful night of stargazing marked overcoming his fear of the dark.
7.20	It deepened his love for astronomy	Facing his fear affected Lucas by deepening his love for astronomy.
7.21	Competitive and dismissive	Initially, Anna was competitive and often dismissive of her peers in the orchestra.
7.22	By emphasizing teamwork in music	Mr. Ellis influenced Anna by emphasizing teamwork and the beauty of collaborative music.
7.23	She valued her peers' talents more	Anna's perspective changed to value her fellow musicians' talents more.
7.24	Improved performance and unity	Anna's transformation improved the orchestra's performance and unity.
7.25	Personal and musical growth	Anna gained personal and musical growth from her experience in the orchestra.
7.26	His daring and aggressive style	Jake was known for his daring and aggressive surfing style.
7.27	Taught him patience and strategy	Mia influenced Jake by teaching him the value of patience and strategy in surfing.
7.28	Adapting to the waves and refining techniques	Jake changed his technique to adapt to the waves and refine his approaches.
7.29	Winning the national championship	Jake's new approach helped him win the national surfing championship.
7.30	From reckless to strategic and thoughtful	Jake's character evolved from being reckless to strategic and thoughtful.
7.31	Writing	Lily's hidden talent was writing, which she hesitated to share.
7.32	Her teacher, Mrs. Evans	Lily was encouraged to enter the writing competition by her teacher, Mrs. Evans.
7.33	Gained confidence and won respect	Lily gained confidence and respect from her peers after participating in the competition.
7.34	Winning the competition and earning friendships	Lily won the competition and earned friendships through her story submission.
7.35	From shy to confident and celebrated	Lily transformed from a reserved individual to a confident and celebrated writer.
7.36	His intelligence and impatience	Alex was known for his intelligence but was often impatient and dismissive.
7.37	Collaborating with a diverse team	Working with a diverse team of developers changed Alex's attitude towards teamwork.
7.38	His dismissiveness of others' ideas	Alex initially caused conflict due to his dismissive approach to others' ideas.
7.39	The value of different perspectives and teamwork	Alex learned to value different perspectives and the importance of teamwork.
7.40	An award for innovation	The team's project won an award for innovation, highlighting the power of collaboration.

Topic 8 – Critical Reading of Diverse Texts

In the ancient city of Mythica, a legendary library held a vast collection of mystical texts. Among them was a rare book, said to contain the secrets of the universe. Many scholars attempted to decipher it, but its language was enigmatic. A young apprentice named Theo, known for his curiosity and perseverance, took on the challenge. He spent days studying the book, exploring the library's archives for clues. Through his analysis, Theo uncovered that the book was not a literal guide, but a series of metaphors representing life's journey. This revelation not only enlightened the scholars but also inspired them to look beyond the surface of texts.

8.1) What was unique about the book in the library of Mythica?

☐ It contained secrets of the universe

☐ It had pages made of gold

☐ It was written by a famous king

☐ It was the oldest book in the world

8.2) What was the challenge with the book?

☐ It was missing pages

☐ Its language was enigmatic

☐ It was in a foreign language

☐ It was encrypted with codes

8.3) How did Theo approach the task of deciphering the book?

☐ Using technology to translate

☐ Studying and exploring library archives

☐ Using a magic spell

☐ Asking experts for help

8.4) What did Theo discover about the book?

☐ It was a fictional story

☐ It was a series of metaphors

☐ It contained a hidden treasure map

☐ It was a historical record

8.5) What impact did Theo's discovery have?

☐ Enlightened scholars to look beyond the surface

☐ Sparked a debate about its authenticity

☐ Discouraged further research

☐ Led to the book being discarded

In the futuristic city of Nova Terra, a group of students participated in a virtual reality (VR) educational program. The program simulated historical events, allowing students to experience different periods firsthand. One student, Ria, was particularly captivated by a simulation of the Renaissance. Through her virtual experiences, she explored art, science, and philosophy of that era. Ria's critical analysis of these simulations led her to understand the interconnectedness of different fields and the impact of historical contexts on developments. Her insights from the VR program enhanced her real-world perspective on interdisciplinary learning and historical appreciation.

8.6) What was the educational program in Nova Terra based on?

☐ Historical movies and documentaries

☐ Lectures by historians

☐ Virtual reality simulations of history

☐ Physical textbooks about history

8.7) Which historical period captivated Ria the most?

☐ The Renaissance

☐ The Middle Ages

☐ The Ancient Egyptian era

☐ The Industrial Revolution

8.8) What did Ria explore through the VR simulations?

☐ Art, science, and philosophy of the Renaissance

☐ Military strategies

☐ Ancient languages

☐ Geographical explorations

8.9) What understanding did Ria gain from her VR experiences?

☐ Technical skills in VR technology

☐ Interconnectedness of fields and historical impacts

☐ Methods of ancient construction

☐ Styles of historical clothing

8.10) How did the VR program influence Ria's real-world perspective?

☐ A desire to travel back in time

☐ Enhanced appreciation for interdisciplinary learning

☐ Interest in becoming a VR developer

☐ A decision to become a historian

In the small town of Greenwood, an annual storytelling competition was the highlight of the community. This year, a young girl named Eliza entered with a tale about a mythical forest and its hidden secrets. Her story, rich with vivid descriptions and intriguing characters, captivated the audience. Eliza's narrative skillfully intertwined themes of adventure, friendship, and the importance of nature conservation. As the story unfolded, listeners were drawn into the magical world she created, leaving them with a deeper understanding of the balance between humans and nature. Eliza's storytelling not only won her the competition but also sparked conversations about environmental awareness in the town.

8.11) What was Eliza's story about in the competition?

☐ A journey to outer space

☐ A historical battle

☐ A mythical forest and its secrets

☐ A futuristic city

8.12) What themes were present in Eliza's story?

☐ Romance, mystery, and technology

☐ Comedy, drama, and family

☐ Adventure, friendship, and nature conservation

☐ Sports, competition, and teamwork

8.13) How did the audience react to Eliza's story?

☐ Confused by the complex plot

☐ Amused by the humorous content

☐ Uninterested and distracted

☐ Captivated by the magical world

8.14) What impact did Eliza's storytelling have on the community?

☐ Sparked environmental awareness conversations

☐ Increased interest in literature

☐ Promoted local tourism

☐ Encouraged more storytelling events

8.15) What did Eliza achieve through her storytelling?

☐ Receiving a scholarship

☐ Becoming a professional writer

☐ Getting her story published

☐ Winning the competition and recognition

In the bustling city of Newhaven, a group of students embarked on a project to create a digital time capsule. The capsule was to capture the essence of their city's culture, history, and aspirations. Each student contributed unique content, from photographs and essays to music and interviews with local figures. As they compiled the capsule, they critically analyzed each piece, discussing its significance and representation of their city. The project not only deepened their understanding of Newhaven's identity but also highlighted the diversity and dynamism of urban life. The time capsule, once completed, was shared online, garnering attention and appreciation from far beyond their city.

8.16) What was the project undertaken by the students in Newhaven?

☐ Organizing a cultural festival

☐ Creating a digital time capsule

☐ Designing a new city monument

☐ Writing a city guidebook

8.17) What types of content did students contribute to the time capsule?

☐ Photos, essays, music, and interviews

☐ Sports achievements and trophies

☐ Blueprints, maps, and science projects

☐ Recipes, clothing designs, and poems

8.18) What did the students do as they compiled the time capsule?

☐ Exchanged items with other schools

☐ Displayed them in a museum

☐ Sold the pieces for fundraising

☐ Analyzed the significance of each piece

8.19) What understanding did the project foster about Newhaven?

☐ Its identity, diversity, and dynamism

☐ Its economic challenges

☐ Its political history

☐ Its environmental issues

8.20) What was the outcome of the time capsule project?

☐ Preserved in a city archive

☐ Transformed into a book

☐ Presented to the city council

☐ Shared online and received wide appreciation

In the serene village of Oakdale, a local library hosted a summer reading challenge for young readers. Among the participants was a twelve-year-old girl named Grace, who was an avid reader but often struggled with interpreting complex themes. The challenge included a variety of genres, from mystery novels to historical fiction. Grace took this as an opportunity to improve her critical reading skills. As she progressed through the books, she engaged in discussions with librarians and peers, gradually enhancing her ability to understand and analyze the underlying themes. By the end of the summer, Grace not only completed the challenge but also developed a deeper appreciation for diverse literature and its insights into human experiences.

8.21) What was the summer challenge at the Oakdale library?

☐ A storytelling contest

☐ A reading challenge with diverse genres

☐ A library renovation project

☐ A book writing competition

8.22) What difficulty did Grace face with reading?

☐ Interpreting complex themes

☐ Finding interesting books

☐ Understanding different languages

☐ Reading quickly

8.23) How did Grace work on improving her critical reading skills?

☐ Writing book reviews

☐ Taking a reading course

☐ Discussing books with librarians and peers

☐ Memorizing book passages

8.24) What was the outcome of Grace's participation in the challenge?

☐ Enhanced understanding and analysis of themes

☐ Becoming a librarian assistant

☐ Starting her own book club

☐ Winning a prize for most books read

8.25) What deeper appreciation did Grace develop?

☐ For classical music

☐ For diverse literature and human experiences

☐ For modern technology in libraries

☐ For writing poetry

In the bustling city of Centerville, a high school history club embarked on a project to create a documentary about the city's heritage. The club, led by an enthusiastic student named Omar, researched various historical periods and interviewed local historians and residents. As they delved into the city's past, they uncovered stories of resilience, innovation, and community spirit. The documentary combined old photographs, narrations, and reenactments, providing a comprehensive view of Centerville's evolution. This project not only enhanced the students' research and analytical skills but also fostered a stronger connection with their city's history.

8.26) What was the high school history club's project in Centerville?

☐ Writing a book on local history

☐ Organizing a historical tour

☐ Restoring a historical landmark

☐ Creating a documentary about the city's heritage

8.27) Who led the research for the documentary?

☐ A student named Omar

☐ A local historian

☐ A professional filmmaker

☐ The school principal

8.28) What themes emerged from the city's history?

☐ Cultural festivals and traditions

☐ War, peace, and politics

☐ Resilience, innovation, and community

☐ Economic growth and decline

8.29) How did the students present Centerville's history?

☐ Old photos, narrations, and reenactments

☐ Paintings and sculptures

☐ Graphs, charts, and statistics

☐ Interviews only

8.30) What skills did the students enhance through this project?

☐ Research and analytical skills

☐ Public speaking and debate

☐ Acting and directing

☐ Graphic design and editing

In the vibrant city of Rivertown, a local theater group decided to adapt a well-known novel into a play. The novel, set in the 19th century, depicted the struggles and triumphs of a family during that era. The adaptation process was led by a creative teenager, Sofia, who was passionate about bringing the story to life on stage. She worked with the actors to interpret the complex characters and their motivations, ensuring the play remained true to the novel's spirit. Through rehearsals and discussions, Sofia and the group explored themes of resilience, societal norms, and family dynamics. The final production was a resounding success, offering a fresh perspective on the timeless story.

8.31) What project did the Rivertown theater group undertake?

☐ Producing a historical documentary

☐ Adapting a novel into a play

☐ Writing an original screenplay

☐ Creating a musical album

8.32) Who led the adaptation of the novel?

☐ The theater director

☐ A professional playwright

☐ A famous actor

☐ A teenager named Sofia

8.33) What was the focus of Sofia's work with the actors?

☐ Interpreting characters and motivations

☐ Learning dance routines

☐ Designing costumes and sets

☐ Improving their singing skills

8.34) What themes were explored in the play?

□ Science, innovation, and progress

□ Romance, betrayal, and revenge

□ Adventure, exploration, and discovery

□ Resilience, societal norms, and family dynamics

8.35) How was the final production of the play received?

□ With mixed reviews and criticism

□ With minimal interest and low attendance

□ As a resounding success with a fresh perspective

□ As an average performance

In the small coastal town of Seabreeze, a local museum curated an exhibit showcasing the maritime history of the region. A group of students, led by an insightful girl named Nora, volunteered to guide visitors through the exhibit. Nora's deep interest in history helped her provide rich explanations of the artifacts, stories of sea voyages, and the town's fishing heritage. She encouraged visitors to think critically about the impact of maritime activities on the town's development and culture. This experience not only broadened the students' historical knowledge but also enhanced their ability to engage others in meaningful discussions about the past.

8.36) What was the focus of the Seabreeze museum exhibit?

□ Artistic achievements of local artists

□ Technological advancements

□ Maritime history of the region

□ Local wildlife and ecosystems

8.37) Who led the student group guiding the exhibit?

☐ A history teacher

☐ A professional tour guide

☐ A museum curator

☐ Nora, a girl interested in history

8.38) What did Nora emphasize in her explanations?

☐ Rich details of artifacts and sea voyages

☐ Economic data on fishing

☐ Technical aspects of shipbuilding

☐ Stories of famous sailors

8.39) What critical aspect did Nora encourage visitors to consider?

☐ Environmental concerns

☐ Future of coastal towns

☐ Impact of maritime activities on the town

☐ Modern challenges in maritime industries

8.40) How did the experience affect the students?

☐ Motivated them to start a conservation project

☐ Enhanced historical knowledge and discussion skills

☐ Led them to plan a sea voyage

☐ Inspired them to study marine biology

Topic 8 – Answers

Question Number	Answer	Explanation
8.1	It contained secrets of the universe	The book in the library of Mythica was unique because it was said to contain the secrets of the universe.
8.2	Its language was enigmatic	The challenge with the book was that its language was enigmatic and difficult to decipher.
8.3	Studying and exploring library archives	Theo approached deciphering the book by studying and exploring the library's archives for clues.
8.4	It was a series of metaphors	Theo discovered that the book was a series of metaphors representing life's journey.
8.5	Enlightened scholars to look beyond the surface	Theo's discovery enlightened scholars to look beyond the surface of texts.
8.6	Virtual reality simulations of history	The educational program in Nova Terra was based on virtual reality simulations of historical events.
8.7	The Renaissance	Ria was particularly captivated by a simulation of the Renaissance period.
8.8	Art, science, and philosophy of the Renaissance	Through the VR simulations, Ria explored art, science, and philosophy of the Renaissance era.
8.9	Interconnectedness of fields and historical impacts	Ria gained an understanding of the interconnectedness of different fields and the impact of historical contexts on developments.
8.10	Enhanced appreciation for interdisciplinary learning	The VR program influenced Ria's real-world perspective by enhancing her appreciation for interdisciplinary learning.
8.11	A mythical forest and its secrets	Eliza's story in the competition was about a mythical forest and its hidden secrets.
8.12	Adventure, friendship, and nature conservation	Eliza's story contained themes of adventure, friendship, and the importance of nature conservation.
8.13	Captivated by the magical world	The audience was captivated by the magical world created in Eliza's story.
8.14	Sparked environmental awareness conversations	Eliza's storytelling sparked conversations about environmental awareness in the community.
8.15	Winning the competition and recognition	Eliza achieved winning the competition and gaining recognition through her storytelling.
8.16	Creating a digital time capsule	The students in Centerville undertook a project to create a digital time capsule.
8.17	Photos, essays, music, and interviews	Students contributed a variety of content to the time capsule, including photos, essays, music, and interviews.
8.18	Analyzed the significance of each piece	As they compiled the time capsule, the students critically analyzed the significance of each piece.

8.19	Its identity, diversity, and dynamism	The project fostered an understanding of Newhaven's identity, diversity, and dynamism.
8.20	Shared online and received wide appreciation	The outcome of the time capsule project was that it was shared online and received wide appreciation.
8.21	A reading challenge with diverse genres	The summer challenge at the Oakdale library was a reading challenge involving a variety of genres.
8.22	Interpreting complex themes	Grace faced difficulty with interpreting complex themes in her reading.
8.23	Discussing books with librarians and peers	Grace worked on improving her critical reading skills by discussing books with librarians and peers.
8.24	Enhanced understanding and analysis of themes	The outcome of Grace's participation in the challenge was an enhanced understanding and analysis of themes.
8.25	For diverse literature and human experiences	Grace developed a deeper appreciation for diverse literature and its insights into human experiences.
8.26	Creating a documentary about the city's heritage	The high school history club's project in Centerville was creating a documentary about the city's heritage.
8.27	A student named Omar	Omar, a student, led the research for the documentary.
8.28	Resilience, innovation, and community	Themes of resilience, innovation, and community emerged from the city's history.
8.29	Old photos, narrations, and reenactments	The students presented Centerville's history using old photographs, narrations, and reenactments.
8.30	Research and analytical skills	The students enhanced their research and analytical skills through this project.
8.31	Adapting a novel into a play	The Rivertown theater group undertook a project to adapt a well-known novel into a play.
8.32	A teenager named Sofia	Sofia, a teenager, led the adaptation of the novel for the play.
8.33	Interpreting characters and motivations	Sofia focused on working with the actors to interpret complex characters and their motivations.
8.34	Resilience, societal norms, and family dynamics	The play explored themes of resilience, societal norms, and family dynamics.
8.35	As a resounding success with a fresh perspective	The final production of the play was received as a resounding success, offering a fresh perspective on the story.
8.36	Maritime history of the region	The focus of the Seabreeze museum exhibit was the maritime history of the region.
8.37	Nora, a girl interested in history	Nora, a girl with a deep interest in history, led the student group guiding the exhibit.
8.38	Rich details of artifacts and sea voyages	Nora emphasized rich details of artifacts, stories of sea voyages, and the town's fishing heritage.
8.39	Impact of maritime activities on the town	Nora encouraged visitors to consider the impact of maritime activities on the town's development and culture.
8.40	Enhanced historical knowledge and discussion skills	The experience enhanced the students' historical knowledge and their ability to engage others in discussions about the past.

ALEXANDER-GRACE EDUCATION

Ready for More?

The NWEA MAP testing is adaptive. This means that if your student found these questions too tricky or too easy, they may find it useful to practice grades below or above they grade they are in. This will expose students to new concepts and ideas, giving them a better chance at scoring higher in tests.

Alexander-Grace Education produces books covering Mathematics, Sciences, and English, to help your student maximize their potential in these areas.

For errata, please email
alexandergraceeducation@gmail.com

ALEXANDER-GRACE EDUCATION

Made in the USA
Las Vegas, NV
30 November 2024